ANNOUNCING THE HAVERGAL EDITION
NOW IN PREPARATION FOR PUBLICATION

The edition of *The Complete Works of Frances Ridley Havergal* has five parts:

Volume I *Behold Your King:*
   The Complete Poetical Works of Frances Ridley Havergal

Volume II *Whose I Am and Whom I Serve:*
   Prose Works of Frances Ridley Havergal

Volume III *Loving Messages for the Little Ones:*
   Works for Children by Frances Ridley Haver

Volume IV *Love for Love: Frances Ridley Havergal:*
   Memorials, Letters and Biographical Works

Volume V *Songs of Truth and Love:*
   Music by Frances Ridley Havergal and William Henry Havergal

David L. Chalkley, Editor   Dr. Glen T. Wegge, Music Editor

The Music of Frances Ridley Havergal by Glen T. Wegge, Ph.D.

This Companion Volume to the Havergal edition is a valuable presentation of F.R.H.'s extant scores. Except for a very few of her hymn scores published in hymn-books, most or nearly all of F.R.H.'s scores have been very little—if any at all—seen, or even known of, for nearly a century. What a valuable body of music has been un-known for so long and is now made available to many. Dr. Wegge completed his Ph.D. in Music Theory at Indiana University at Bloomington, and his diligence and thoroughness in this volume are obvious. First an analysis of F.R.H.'s compositions is given, an essay that both addresses the most advanced musicians and also reach-es those who are untrained in music; then all the extant scores that have been found are newly typeset, with complete texts for each score and extensive indices at the end of the book. This volume presents F.R.H.'s music in newly typeset scores diligently prepared by Dr. Wegge, and Volume V of the Havergal edition presents the scores in facsimile, the original 19th century scores. (The essay—a dissertation—analysing her scores is given the same both in this Companion Volume and in Volume V of the Havergal edition.)

Dr. Wegge is also preparing all of these scores for publication in performance fo-lio editions.

A sinking ship in a storm at sea.

"'Now!"

I.

A NIGHT of danger on the sea,
  Of sleeplessness and fear!
Wave after wave comes thundering
  Against the strong stone pier;
Each with a terrible recoil,
  And a grim and gathering might,
As blast on blast comes howling past,
Each wild gust wilder than the last,
  All through that awful night.

II.

Well for the ships in the harbour now,
  Which came with the morning tide;
With unstrained cable and anchor sure,
  How quietly they ride!
Well for the barque that reached at eve,
  Though watched with breathless fear,
It was sheltered first ere the tempest burst,
  It is safe inside the pier!

III.

But see! a faint and fatal light
  Out on the howling sea!
'Tis a vessel that seeks the harbour mouth,
  As in death-agony.
Though the strong stone arms are open wide,
  She has missed the only way;
'Tis all too late, for the storm drives fast,
The mighty waves have swept her past,
And against that sheltering pier shall cast
  Their wrecked and shattered prey.

IV.

Nearer and nearer the barque is borne,
    As over the deck they dash,
Where sailors five are clinging fast
To the sailless stump of the broken mast,
    Waiting the final crash.
Is it all too late? is there succour yet
    Those perishing men to reach?
Life is so near on the firm-built pier,
    That else must be death to each.

V.

There are daring hearts and powerful arms,
    And swift and steady feet,
And they rush as down to a yawning grave,
In the strong recoil of the mightiest wave,
Treading that awful path to save,
    As they trod a homeward street.
Over the boulders and foam they rush
    Into the ghastly hollow;
They fling the rope to the heaving wreck,
The aim was sure, and it strikes the deck,
    As the shouts of quick hope follow.

VI.

Reached, but not saved! there is more to
    A trumpet note is heard;   [do,
And over the rage and over the roar
Of billowy thunders on the shore,
    Rings out the guiding word.
There is one chance, and only one,
    All can be saved, but how?
'The rope hold fast, but quit the mast
    At the trumpet-signal "NOW!"'

VII.

There is a moment when the sea
    Has spent its furious strength;
A shuddering pause with a sudden swirl,
Gathering force again to hurl
Billow on billow in whirl on whirl;
    That moment comes at length—
With a single shout the '*Now*' peals out,
    And the answering leap is made.
Well for the simple hearts that just
Loosing the mast with fearless trust,
    The strange command obeyed!

VIII.

For the rope is good, and the stout arms
    Ere the brief storm-lull is o'er; [pull
It is but a swift and blinding sweep
Through the waters wild and dark and
    And the men are safe on shore— [deep,
Safe! though the fiend-like blast pursue,
    Safe! though the waves dash high;
But the ringing cheer that rises clear
    Is pierced with a sudden cry:

IX.

'There are but four drawn up to shore,
    And five were on the deck!'
And the straining gaze that conquers
Still traces, drifting on to doom, [gloom
    One man upon the wreck.
Again they chase in sternest race
The far-recoiling wave;
    The rope is thrown to the tossing
But reaches not in the windy dark [mark
    The one they strive to save.

X.

Again they rush, and again they fail,
　Again, and yet again:
The storm yells back defiance loud,
The breakers rear a rampart proud,
　And roar, 'In vain, in vain!'

XI.

Then a giant wave caught up the wreck,
　And bore it on its crest;
One moment it hung quivering there
　In horrible arrest.
And the lonely man on the savage sea
　A lightning flash uplit,
Still clinging fast to the broken mast
　That he had not dared to quit.

XII.

Then horror of great darkness fell,
　While eyes flashed inward fire;
And over all the roar and dash,
Through that great blackness came a crash,
　A token sure and dire.
The wave had burst upon the pier,
　The wreck was scattered wide;
Another 'Now' would never reach
The corpse that lay upon the beach
　With the receding tide.

XIII.

God's 'Now' is sounding in your ears;
　Oh, let it reach your heart!
Not only from your sinfulness
　He bids you part;
Your righteousness as filthy rags
　Must all relinquished be,
And only Jesus' precious death
　Must be your plea.

XIV.

Now trust the one provided rope,
　Now quit the broken mast,
Before the hope of safety be
　For ever past.
Fear not to trust His simple word,
　So sweet, so tried, so true,
And you are safe for evermore;
　Yes,—even you!

F.R.H.

Come unto Me, all ye that labor and are heavy laden, and I will give you rest. Take My yoke upon you, and learn of Me, for I am meek and lowly in heart, and ye shall find rest unto your souls. For My yoke is easy, and My burden is light.

Matthew 11:28–30

And the Spirit and the bride say, Come. And let him that heareth say, Come. And let him that is athirst come. And whosoever will, let him take the water of life freely.

Revelation 22:17

Love for Love.

1 JOHN 4:16.

KNOWING that the God on high,
  With a tender Father's grace,
Waits to hear your faintest cry,
  Waits to show a Father's face,—
Stay and think!—oh, should not you
Love this gracious Father too?

Knowing Christ was crucified,
  Knowing that He loves you now
Just as much as when He died
  With the thorns upon His brow,—
Stay and think!—oh, should not you
Love this blessèd Saviour too?

Knowing that a Spirit strives
  With your weary, wandering heart,
Who can change the restless lives,
  Pure and perfect peace impart,—
Stay and think!—oh, should not you
Love this loving Spirit too?

Frances Ridley Havergal

THE

ROYAL INVITATION.

DAILY THOUGHTS ON COMING TO CHRIST.

BY

FRANCES RIDLEY HAVERGAL.

"Him that cometh to Me I will in no wise cast out."—John 6:37.

"Knowing her intense desire that Christ should be magnified, whether
by her life or in her death, may it be to His glory
that in these pages she, being dead,
'Yet speaketh ! ' "

Taken from the Edition of *The Complete Works of Frances Ridley Havergal.*

David L. Chalkley, Editor   Dr. Glen T. Wegge, Associate Editor

ISBN 978-1-937236-09-0   Library of Congress: 2011939761

Book cover by Sherry Goodwin and David Carter.

CONTENTS.

Note: "The Consummation of the Invitation" was the end of *The Royal Invitation*. These next items were not published in that book, but are added in this new edition:

The Royal Invitation, published by Frances in 1878, had no frontispiece nor illustrations. The frontispiece of a ship sinking in a storm at sea was the frontispiece of *Never Say Die* by Samuel Gillespie Prout, a book addressed to unsaved people and pointing them to the Savior, that F.R.H. edited for publication and so strongly recommended to be widely known and used.

This next piece was published in a collection entitled *The Traveller's Guide from Death to Life* (London: S. W. Partridge & Co., no date, likely 1880 to 1900).

"I DO NOT FEAR DEATH."

Extract from F. R. H.'s MS., in answer to a remark: "Death, which we ALL dread."

No, not "All!" One who has seen and *accepted* God's way of salvation, does *not* dread death. Perhaps I shall best express myself by doing it very personally —just giving my own experience.

I do not fear death. Often I wake in the night and think of it, look forward to it, with a thrill of joyful expectation and anticipation, which would become impatience, were it not that Jesus is my Master, as well as my Saviour, and I feel I have work to do for Him that I would not shirk, and also that *His* time to call me home will be the *best* and *right* time; therefore I am content to wait.

One night I was conscious of certain symptoms preluding an all but fatal attack (of erysipelas) I had had once before on the brain.

I knew, if means failed, it was probably my last night on earth. I let my mother attend to me, but alarmed no one, and I was left alone in bed. Then, alone in the dark, I felt it might be my last conscious hour on earth, and that either sleep or fatal unconsciousness would set in. I never spent a calmer, sweeter hour than that. I had not one shadow of fear! only happy rest and confidence in Him "Whom I have believed."

Was this delusion? Could it be so in the very face of death, that great *unmasker* of all uncertainties? I knew it was not delusion, for "I know Whom I have believed."

It was not always thus. I know as well as any one, what it is to "*dread death*," and to put away the thought of its absolute certainty, because I dare not look it in the face.

There was a time when I saw clearly I could *not* save myself—that I deserved hell in many ways, but in one most of all, this—that I owed the whole love of my heart to God, and had not given it to Him; that Jesus had *so* loved me as to *die for me,* and yet I had treated Him with daily, hourly ingratitude. I had broken the first commandment, and as I owed all my life—future and past—to God, I had literally "*nothing to pay*"; for living to Him, and keeping His commands for the future, would not atone for the past. I saw the sinfulness of my heart and life. I could not make my heart better. "*The soul that sinneth it shall die.*" So, unless sin *is* taken away, my soul *must die and go to hell.*

Where then was my hope? In the same Word of God (1 John 5:10), it is written, "He that believeth on the Son hath the witness in himself," and (John 3:36), "He that believeth on the Son *hath everlasting life:* and he that believeth *not* the Son shall not see life; but the *wrath* of God abideth on Him."

Believe what?—that He *must* keep His word and punish sin, and that He *has* punished it in the person of Jesus, *our Substitute,* "Who His own self bare our sins in His own body on the tree" (1 Peter 2:24).

If Jesus has paid *my* debt, and borne the punishment of *my* sins, I simply accept this, and believe Him, and it is all a true and real transaction. I did this—I believed it, and cast myself, utterly hopeless and helpless in myself, at the feet of Jesus, took Him at His word, and accepted what He had done for me.

Result?—Joy, peace in believing, and a happy, FULL trust in Him, which death cannot touch.

Now it is a reality of realities to me—it is so intertwined with my life, that I know nothing could separate me from His love.

I could not do without Jesus. I cannot and I do not live without Him. It is a *new* and different life; and the life and light which takes away *all fear of death,* is what I want others to have and enjoy.

"Death is swallowed up in *victory.* O death, where is thy sting? O grave, where is thy victory? The sting of death is sin; and the strength of sin is the law. But thanks be to God, which giveth us the victory through our Lord Jesus Christ" (1 Cor. 15:54–57).

F.R.H.

———— ❧ ————

"*Just as I am.*"

"Him that cometh unto Me I will in no wise cast out." John 6:37

Just as I am—without one plea
But that Thy blood was shed for me,
And that Thou bid'st me come to Thee—
　　　O Lamb of God, I come!

Just as I am—and waiting not
To rid my soul of one dark blot,
To Thee, whose blood can cleanse each
　　spot—
　　　O Lamb of God, I come!

Just as I am, though toss'd about,
With many a conflict, many a doubt,
Fightings and fears within, without—
　　　O Lamb of God, I come!

Just as I am—poor, wretched, blind;
Sight, riches, healing of the mind,
Yea, all I need, in Thee I find—
　　　O Lamb of God, I come!

Just as I am—Thou wilt receive,
Wilt welcome, pardon, cleanse, relieve,
Because Thy promise I believe—
　　　O Lamb of God, I come!

Just as I am—Thy love unknown
Has broken every barrier down;
Now to be Thine, yea, Thine alone—
　　　O Lamb of God, I come!

Just as I am—of that free love,
The breadth, length, depth, and height to prove,
Here, for a season, then above—
　　　O Lamb of God, I come!

Charlotte Elliott

Jesus, I will trust Thee, trust Thee with my soul;
Guilty, lost, and helpless, Thou canst make me whole.
There is none in heaven or on earth like Thee.
Thou hast died for sinners—therefore, Lord, for me.

Jesus, I may trust Thee, name of matchless worth
Spoken by the angel at Thy wondrous birth;
Written, and for ever, on Thy cross of shame,
Sinners read and worship, trusting in that name.

Jesus, I must trust Thee, pondering Thy ways,
Full of love and mercy all Thine earthly days:
Sinners gathered round Thee, lepers sought Thy face—
None too vile or loathsome for a Saviour's grace.

Jesus, I can trust Thee, trust Thy written word,
Though Thy voice of pity I have never heard.
When Thy Spirit teacheth, to my taste how sweet—
Only may I hearken, sitting at Thy feet.

Jesus, I do trust Thee, trust without a doubt:
"Whosoever cometh, Thou wilt not cast out."
Faithful is Thy promise, precious is Thy blood—
These my soul's salvation, Thou my Saviour God!　　Mary Jane Walker

FIRST DAY.

The Giver of the Invitation.

"Come unto Me."—Matthew 11:28.

THIS is the Royal Invitation. For it is given by the King of kings. We are so familiar with the words, that we fail to realize them. May the Holy Spirit open our ear that we may hear the voice of our King in them, and that they may reach our souls with imperative power. Then, "they shall know in that day that I am He that doth speak."

"Lord, to whom shall we go?" Not "to *what* shall we go?" For the human heart within us craves a personal, living rest and refuge. No doctrines, however true; no systems, however perfect; nothing mental, moral, or spiritual, will do as the answer to this question of every soul that is not absolutely dead in trespasses and sins. As surely as you and I are persons, individualities, real separate existences, so surely must we have a Person, no less real and individual, to whom to go in our more or less conscious need of salvation. And so the great word of Invitation, Royal and Divine, is given to us, "Come unto ME!"

"Unto *Me*." Just think what that one word means! Seek out all the great and wonderful titles of Christ for yourself, and write after each one—"And *He* says, Come unto *Me!*" Unto Me, "the mighty God," nothing less than that! "Mighty to save" and "ready to save me."

Then seek out all the exquisitely winning beauties of the character and words and ways of Him who went about doing good, till you "have heard Him and observed Him" all through those years of patient and perfect ministry, and recollect all the time that it is *He* who says to you, "Come unto *Me!*" Unto Him, the man Christ Jesus, full of compassion, and tender yet royal grace.

John 10:27
1 Thess. 1:5
Isaiah 52:6
John 6:68

Psalm 142:5

Ephesians 2:1

Isaiah 9:6; 63:1
Isaiah 38:20

Acts 10:38
Hosea 14:8
Matthew 20:28

1 Tim. 2:5; Matt. 14:14, etc.; Jn 1:14

1 Peter 2:24
Isaiah 53:6
John 13:1
Song. 8:6
Isa. 40:9; Jn. 19:5
Gal. 2:20; Isaiah
65:1; Heb. 12:2
Mk. 4:19; Jn. 1:29

Lament. 1:12
Revelation 22:16,
17

Hebrews 12:25
Rev. 1:7; Acts
10:42; 1 Peter 3:22
Luke 11:23
Isaiah 65:2
Matthew 22:5

Revelation 20:11
Matthew 25:31
Matthew 25:32
Acts 1:11

Then look at the great central scene of the universe,—the central moment not of a world's history only, but of eternity;—look at the Saviour, who His own self bare our sins in His own body on the tree, bowing His bleeding head under that awful burden, because His faithfulness was unto the death, and His love was strong as death! "Behold your God," and "Behold the Man," who loved you and gave Himself for you; hear His own touching call, "I said, Behold Me, behold Me!" Look away from all the "other things," look at the Crucified One, and, as you gaze, remember that *He* says, "Come unto Me!"

Is it nothing to you, all ye that pass by, that both from the depth of sorrow and from the height of glory this Royal Invitation comes to you?

For it is the call not only of Jesus Crucified, but of Jesus Reigning and Jesus Coming. "See that ye refuse not Him that speaketh," for He is coming to judge the quick and the dead. He is reigning now, and there are no neutrals in His kingdom. All are either willing and loyal subjects, or actual rebels,—those who have obeyed the King's call, and come, and those who have "made light of it," and *not* come.

Which are you?

Think of the day when the great white throne is set, and when the Son of man shall come in His glory; when all will be gathered before Him, and He shall separate them one from another, and know that it is "this same Jesus" who now says to you, "Come unto *Me!*"

Just as I am—without one plea,
But that Thy blood was shed for me,
And that Thou bidd'st me come to Thee,
O Lamb of God, I come!

SECOND DAY.

What Is "Coming"?

"Come unto Me."—Matthew 11:28.

"**B**UT what is 'coming'?"
One's very familiarity with the terms used to express spiritual things, seems to have a tendency to make one feel mystified about them. And their very simplicity makes one suspicious, as it were, that there must be some mysterious and mystical meaning behind them, because they sound *too* easy and plain to have such great import. "Come" means "come,"—just that! and not some occult process of mental effort.

What would you understand by it, if you heard it today for the first time, never having had any doubts or suppositions or previous notions whatever about it? What does a little child understand by it? It is positively too simple to be made plainer by any amount of explanation. If you could see the Lord Jesus standing there, right before you, and you heard Him say, "Come!" would you say, "What does "come" mean?" And if the room were dark, so that you could only hear and not see, would it make any difference? Would you not turn instantly towards the "Glorious Voice"? Would you not, in heart, and will, and intention, instantaneously obey it?—that is, if you *believed* it to be Himself. For "he that cometh to God must believe that He is." The coming so hinges on that, as to be really the same thing. The moment you really believed, you would really come; and the moment you really come, you really believe. Now the Lord Jesus is as truly and actually "nigh thee" as if you could see Him. And He as truly and actually says "Come" to you as if you heard Him. Fear not, believe only, and *let* yourself come to Him straight away! "Take

Margin references: 1 Cor. 2:10; Matthew 11:25; Proverbs 8:9; Revelation 3:20; Matthew 14:29; Isaiah 30:30; Jeremiah 3:22; Hebrews 11:6; John 6:35; Deut. 30:14; Luke 8:50; Hosea 14:2

John 6:37

Matt. 8:2, 5, 25
Matt. 9:10, 14,
18, 20, 28
Matt. 14:29
Matt. 15:22, etc.
Matt. 28:5
John 12:21; 3:26
Lk. 11:13; Ps. 63:1
John 12:32
John 4:42

1 John 4:14
John 20:28

with you words, and turn to the Lord: say unto Him, Take away all iniquity, and receive us graciously." And know that His answer is, "Him that cometh to Me, I will in no wise cast out."

Do you still feel unaccountably puzzled about it? Give a quiet hour to the records of how others came to Him. Begin with the eighth of St. Matthew, and trace out all through the Gospels how they came to Jesus with all sorts of different needs, and trace in these your own spiritual needs of cleansing, healing, salvation, guidance, sight, teaching. They knew what they wanted, and they knew Whom they wanted. And consequently they just *came*. Ask the Holy Spirit to show you what you want and Whom you want, and you will talk no more about what it means, you will just *come*. And then you will say, "Now we believe, not because of thy saying; for we have heard Him ourselves, and know that this is indeed the Christ, the Saviour of the world"; and you will say, "*My* Lord and *my* God."

THIRD DAY.

All Things Are Ready.

"Come; for all things are now ready."—Luke 14:17.

Isaiah 38:20
John 6:37
Romans 8:9
Hebrews 2:3
Romans 5:11
Hebrews 9:12
Zechariah 13:1
Romans 3:22
Hebrews 10:19,20
1 Timothy 4:8
2 Peter 1:3, 4
Philippians 4:19
Isa. 45:24; 58:11
John 14:26; Psalm
121:3; Acts 22:10;
Eph. 2:10; 1 Peter
5:7; John 14:27;
Isaiah 25:6;
Matthew 22:4

1 Timothy 1:15
John 19:30
John 17:4

1 John 4:14
Daniel 9:24
Deut. 32:4

Eccles. 3:14

*A*LL things! God the Father is ready to save you. Jesus Christ is ready to receive you. The Holy Spirit is ready to dwell in you. Are you ready?

All things. The "great salvation" is ready for you. The full atonement is made for you. The eternal redemption is obtained for you. Are you ready?

All things. The cleansing fountain is opened for you. The robe of righteousness is wrought for you. The way into the holiest is consecrated for you. Are you ready?

All things. All things that pertain unto life and godliness are given you by His Divine power. Exceeding great and precious promises are given you. The supply of all your need is guaranteed to you. Strength and guidance, teaching and keeping, are provided for you. Even the good works in which you shall walk are prepared for you. A Father's love and care and a Saviour's gift of peace are waiting for you. The feast is spread for you. All these things are ready for you. Are you ready for them?

Even if you did not heed nor believe any other words of Jesus, could you—*can* you—doubt His dying words? Surely they are worthy of all acceptation! What are they?

"IT IS FINISHED!"

What is finished? "I have finished the work that Thou gavest Me to do." And what is that work? Simply the work of our salvation. That is the reason why all things are now ready, because Jesus has finished that all-inclusive work. When a thing is finished, how much is there left to do? The question sounds too absurd with respect to ordinary things. We hardly take the trouble to answer, "Why, nothing, of course!" When Jesus has finished the work, how much

Acts 16:30, 31
Acts 13:39
2 Timothy 2:13

Jn 16:31; Mk 9:24
Revelation 1:5
Psalm 45:2
1 Peter 2:22
John 6:47

Acts 8:32–39
John 3:16
John 3:36
John 6:35

John 9:35, 38
Romans 6:23
2 Cor. 9:15
Colossians 1:12
Isaiah 12:1, 2
Ps. 9:1; 1 Pet. 2:9
Rev. 5:9–12

is there left for you to do? Do you not see? *Nothing*, of course! You have only to accept that work as really finished, and accept His dying declaration that it is so. What further assurance would you have? Is not this enough? Does your heart say Yes, or No?

"Do ye now believe?" Settle that; and then what follows? Hear another word of the Faithful Witness. Remember, it is no less true than the other. The holy Lips that spoke that grand truth on the cross spoke nothing that could deceive or mislead. "Verily, verily, I say unto you, He that believeth on Me hath everlasting life." What does this mean? Just what it says, and nothing less! It means that even if you never believed before—even if you never had a spark of faith or glimmer of hope before—yet if you have now given your heart-assent to Jesus and His finished work, you have now everlasting life! That heart-assent is believing; and "he that believeth on the Son hath everlasting life." And this "believing" is "coming"; and thus coming you shall find for yourself that all things are indeed ready.

What now? Shall praise be the only thing not ready? Will you not now prove your acceptance of the great gift of eternal life by pouring out your thanks at once for it, and prove your trust in the finished work by praising the Saviour who died to finish it for you?

> From the cross uplifted high,
> Where the Saviour deigns to die,
> What melodious sounds I hear,
> Bursting on my ravished ear!
> Love's redeeming work is done;
> Come, and welcome! sinner, come!
>
> Spread for thee the festal board,
> See with richest dainties stored;
> To thy Father's bosom pressed,
> Yet again a child confessed,
> Never from His house to roam;
> Come, and welcome! sinner, come!

THOMAS HAWEIS.

FOURTH DAY.

Now.

"Come now."—Isaiah 1:18.

Luke 14:17

ALL things are *now* ready, therefore come *now*! Experience does not run on rails laid regularly down, and readers do not always go hand in hand and heart to heart with the writer. I only wish they did! Then we might try

Isaiah 28:10

to lead on more quickly, instead of reiterating the one call, in the hope that it may, first or last, be heard and obeyed. Please do not imagine, because there are twenty-seven more chapters on the same subject, that there is any sort of slow necessary progress, any set of ideas and feelings to be gone or got through, gradually working up to the climax of "coming." This is all cut short by the simple word, "Come *now!*"

2 Cor. 6:2

Nothing can be plainer. Therefore, if you postpone coming, you are calmly disobeying God. When we bid a child to "come," we do not count it obedience unless it comes at once, then and there. It is not obedience if it stops to consider, and coolly tells you it is "really thinking about com-

Romans 10:21

ing," and waits to see how long you will choose to go on calling it.

Jeremiah 7:13
Isaiah 65:2
James 4:14
Hebrews 4:7
Luke 12:20

What right have we to treat our holy Lord as we would not think of letting a naughty child treat us? He says, "Come now." And "now" does not mean tomorrow. "To-day, if ye will hear His voice, harden not your hearts."

Put it to yourself, what if *this night* God should require your soul of you, and you had not "come"? What if the summons finds you still far off, when the Precious Blood

Ephesians 2:13
Proverbs 27:1

was ready, by which you might have been made nigh? You do not know what a day may bring forth. There are plenty of things besides immediate death which may just as effectu-

Hebrews 12:17

ally prevent your ever coming at all if you do not come now.

Proverbs 1:24–26
Matt. 25:10–12
Mark 4:19
Ephesians 4:30
Isaiah 63:10
Psalm 51:11

This might be your last free hour for coming. To-morrow the call may seem rather less urgent, and the "other things entering in" may deaden it, and the grieved Spirit may withdraw and cease to give you even your present inclination to listen to it, and so you may drift on and on, farther and farther from the haven of safety (into which you may enter *now* if you will), till it is out of sight on the horizon. And then it may be too late to turn the helm, and the current may be too strong; and when the storm of mortal illness at last comes, you may find that you are too weak mentally or physically to rouse yourself even to hear, much less to come. What *can* one do when fever or exhaustion are triumphing over mind and body? Do not risk it. Come NOW! And "though your sins be as scarlet, they shall be as white as snow; though they be red like crimson, they shall be as wool."

Isaiah 1:18

FIFTH DAY.

Coming into the Ark.

"Come thou, and all thy house, into the Ark."—Genesis 7:1.

NO need to repeat the story! We knew it all at six years old. To-day the words are sent to you, "Come *thou!*"

We are either inside or outside the Ark. There is no half-way in this. Outside is death, inside is life. Outside is certain, inevitable, utter destruction. Inside is certain and complete safety. Where are you at this moment? Perhaps you dare not say confidently and happily, "I am inside"; and yet you do not like to look the alarming alternative in the face, and say, "I am outside!" And you prefer trying to persuade yourself that you do not exactly know, and can't be expected to be able to answer such a question. And you say, perhaps with a shade of annoyance, "How *am* I to know?" God's infallible Word tells you very plainly, "If any man be *in* Christ, he is a new creature: old things are passed away; behold, all things are become new." "A very severe test!" you say. I cannot help that; I can only tell you exactly what God says. "I cannot reverse it," and you cannot alter it. So then, if old things have *not* passed away in your life, and if you are *not* a new creature, "born again," altogether different in heart and life and love and aim, you are not "in Christ." And if you are not "*in* Christ," you are *out* of Christ, outside the only place of safety.

"Come thou *into* the Ark!" It is one of the devices of the destroyer to delude you into fancying that no very decided step is necessary. He is very fond of the word "gradually." You are to become more earnest—gradually. You are to find salvation—gradually. You are to turn your mind to God—gradually. Did you ever think that God never once

Margin references:
Deut. 30:15–19
John 3:36
1 John 5:10

1 John 2:5
1 John 3:14, 24
1 John 4:13
1 John 5:13

2 Cor. 5:17

Numbers 23:20

Galatians 6:15
John 3:3
1 John 3:14
Eph. 2:12, 13
Acts 4:12

Proverbs 18:10
Acts 16:33
John 5:24

Genesis 7:21, 22
Hebrews 12:25

Isaiah 33:14
Mark 9:44
1 Peter 4:17
Psalm 50:22
2 Thess. 1:7, 8
Matthew 25:10
Luke 13:25–28
Hebrews 12:17
Eccles. 11:3
Revelation 20:12

2 Peter 3:10

Jeremiah 5:31
Revelation 6:17
1 Peter 4:17, 18

Isaiah 32:2
Ps. 143:9; Matt.
3:7; Psalm 32:7
Genesis 6:17

Genesis 7:16

Genesis 7:13
John 10:9
Luke 17:27

Genesis 7:23

uses this word nor anything like it? Neither the word nor the sense of it occurs in any way in the whole Bible with reference to salvation. You might have been "gradually" approaching the Ark, and "gradually" making up your mind to enter; but unless you took the one step *into* the Ark, the one step from outside to inside, what would have been your fate when the door was shut?

"Come *thou* into the Ark!" I want the call to haunt you, to ring in your ears all day and all night, *till you come.*

For at this moment, if you are not *in* the Ark, you are in more awful danger than you can conceive. Just because you know it is so awful, you shut your eyes and try *not* to think of it! But there it is, all the same. Any moment the door may be shut for you. Any hour may be the sunset of your day of grace, with no twilight of possibilities of salvation beyond. And then, as the tree falleth, so it lieth. As death finds you, so the judgment will find you. Where it finds you, inside or outside the Ark, there the day of the Lord will find you, "in the which the heavens shall pass away with a great noise, and the elements shall melt with fervent heat; the earth also, and the works that are therein, shall be burned up." What will you do then, when neither heavens nor earth afford even a standing place for you?

But "come thou *into the Ark!*" Jesus is the Ark. He is the iding-place from that fiery tempest. "I flee unto Thee to hide me" "from the wrath to come." "Thou art my Hiding-place."

He who brings the flood has provided the Ark. And the door is open. It *will* be shut some day—it may be shut tomorrow. What will you do if you find yourself not shut *in*, but shut *out*? Whose fault is it if you do not enter in and be saved?

Noah did not put it off. He and his family entered the self-same day into the Ark. I wonder if any of Noah's acquaintances were thinking about coming when the flood overtook them, and even coming "gradually" nearer! We are told that "Noah *only* remained alive, and they that were with him in the Ark." Then, once more, "*Come* thou into

Joel 2:31
2 Peter 3:14;
Philippians 3:9

the Ark," that when the "great and terrible day" comes, you may be "found of Him in peace," "found *in* Him."

The rising tempest sweeps the sky,
The rain descends, the winds are high:
The waters swell, and death and fear
Beset thy path, no refuge near:
　　Haste, traveller, haste!

Oh, haste! a shelter you may gain,
A covert from the wind and rain,
A hiding-place, a rest, a home,
A refuge from the wrath to come:
　　Haste, traveller, haste!

W. B. COLLYER.

SIXTH DAY.

Drawn into the Ark.

"Thou shalt come into the Ark."—Genesis 6:18.

Romans 5:6

Deut. 32:36

Isaiah 42:8
Isaiah 59:16
John 5:7, 8
Ephesians 2:1
Isaiah 64:7

2 Peter 3:9
1 Timothy 2:4

Song. 1:4

John 5:40

Jeremiah 3:19

Revelation 22:17

YOU would like to take this great step out of danger into safety; but you find it very hard, though it sounds very easy. You feel as if you had spiritual nightmare,—seeing the danger, and not able to stir hand or foot to escape it.

Perhaps every one who comes to Christ has this sense of utter helplessness about it. This is because the Holy Spirit must convince us that the whole thing is God's doing, and not ours, so that He may have *all* the glory of saving us from beginning to end. It is not at all because He is not willing to save us, but just because He *is* willing, that He lets us find out for ourselves that our own will is so numb that it cannot rouse and move without the fire of His love and grace.

Now just trust His promise, "Thou shalt come into the Ark"; in other words, believe that His power and love are even now being exerted upon you, and that your sense of helplessness is only part of His wonderful way of drawing you to Jesus. God the Father is "not willing that any should perish, but that all should come to repentance."

Then why do any perish? Simply because they *won't* come; because they will not yield to the winning love and the "drawing" power which is now being put forth to save you, if, as you read this, you *want* to be saved. There is no sadder word in the Bible than "Ye *will* not come to Me, that ye might have life." But if you are saying, ever so feebly and faintly, "I will," God meets it with His strong and gracious "Thou *shalt.*"

Do not fear to take the "*Thou*" to yourself. Remember the great "Whosoever will," and look up at this star of promise in the dark, "Thou shalt come into the Ark."

Jesus said, "All that the Father giveth Me *shall* come to Me." And the Father says, "I will cause him to draw near, and he shall approach unto Me; for who is this that engaged his heart to approach unto me?" Whose heart? Is it not yours? You would hardly be reading these pages, if your heart were not at all engaged to approach unto Him. And if it is so engaged, who engaged it? Who but the God from whom alone "*all* holy desires do proceed"?

Then go on a few verses farther, and see the word of the Lord to you. "Yea, I have loved thee with an everlasting love; *therefore* with loving-kindness have I drawn thee." Now do not wrong, and wound, and insult that tremendous love by refusing to believe it. He is at this moment giving you the personal proof of it, by "drawing" you even for these few minutes. Do not resist the half-formed wish to come to Jesus. It is very solemn to realize that this is no less than the Father's own drawing of you to His dear Son. Without it you could not come, because you know you would have refused to come; but with it, if only you yield to it, "thou *shalt* come into the Ark."

When the dove found no rest for the sole of her foot, and returned to Noah because the waters were on the face of the whole earth, "then he put forth his hand, and took her, and pulled her in" (margin, "caused her to come") "unto him into the Ark." What a beautiful picture is this little helpless tired dove of our helplessness and weariness, and the kind Hand, strong and tender, which does not leave us to flutter and beat against a closed window, but takes us, and *pulls* us "*unto* Him, *into* the Ark!"

So we have the willingness of the Father in one part of the type, and the willingness of the Son in another part,— willingness to receive you into safety and rest. Then "Come *thou* into the Ark!"

Marginal references:

John 6:37
Jeremiah 30:21

Jeremiah 31:3

Hosea 11:4

John 6:44
Luke 13:34

Genesis 8:9
Isaiah 60:8
Song. 5:2

Luke 14:23

Ezekiel 18:23
2 Cor. 6:17
Luke 15:2
John 12:32
Genesis 7:1

SEVENTH DAY.

———

Coming for Rest.

"Come unto Me, all ye that labour and are heavy laden, and I will give you rest."
—Matthew 11:28.

Micah 2:10
Eccles. 2:17–20
Genesis 8:9

Revelation 14:11

Habakkuk 2:13
Jeremiah 9:5
Isaiah 57:10

Job 16:7

Isaiah 1:4
Isaiah 53:6
John 16:8, 9
Zechariah 13:1
1 John 1:7

Psalm 38:4

Psalm 55:22

"THIS is *not* your rest." God says so, and therefore it is no use seeking or hoping or trying for it. You may as well give up first as last. The dove found no rest for the sole of her foot till she came to the Ark; and neither will you. And the end of the dreary vista of unrest all through the years of a life without Christ, is, "They have no rest day nor night."

"The people shall weary themselves for very vanity." Do you know anything about that? "They weary themselves to commit iniquity." "Thou art wearied in the greatness of thy way." Do these words come home to you? Or, "But now He hath made me weary; Thou hast made desolate all my company"? Whether it is the weariness of sin or of sorrow, of vanity or of desolation (and sooner or later the one must lead into the other), the gentle call floats over the troubled waters, "Come unto Me, all ye that labour" (or "are weary"), "and I will give you rest."

But stay; you may, or rather you must, put in a double claim to the promise. You may not be, consciously, particularly weary or labouring; but whether conscious of it or not, you are heavy laden, unless the one great burden of sin is taken away from you. It is a fact, whether the Holy Spirit has convinced you of it or not as yet, that unless your iniquity is taken away by personal washing in the only Fountain, you are in the position described in the 38th Psalm, "Mine iniquities are gone over my head; as an heavy burden, they are too heavy for me." So much too heavy for you, that if you do not accept Christ's offer of rest from that

Ezek 33:10; Psalm 16:11; 1 Pet. 2:24

Isaiah 14:3

Hebrews 4:3

1 Chron. 22:18
1 Kings 5:4

1 Chron. 22:9
Isaiah 11:10

Isaiah 28:12

Hosea 13:9

Isaiah 30:15

burden, you will never be able to find or follow the path of life. But why bear it one minute longer, when Jesus says, "Come unto Me, all ye that are heavy laden, and I will give you rest"?

"He hath given us rest by *His* sorrow, and life by His death" [John Bunyan]; "rest from *thy* sorrow, and from thy fear, and from thy hard bondage wherein thou wast made to serve." Come and take the gift! It is gloriously real. It is no mere slight and temporary sense of relief. "We which have believed *do* enter into rest."

And He gives us "rest on *every* side,"—complete rest, guarded and sheltered all round.

It is not only rest *from* all the weariness and burdens, but rest *in* Himself. Jesus is spoken of in type as "the Man of Rest," "and His rest shall be glorious." It is this, His own Divine rest, that He will give.

"This is the rest wherewith ye may cause the weary to rest." Is it not worth having? Will you not come for it? You *cannot* have it without coming to Jesus; but only come, and it shall be yours—for there stands His word—and "in returning and rest shall ye be saved."

I heard the voice of Jesus say,
 "Come unto Me and rest;
Lay down, thou weary one, lay down
 Thy head upon My breast."
I came to Jesus as I was,
 Weary, and worn, and sad;
I found in Him a resting-place,
 And He has made me glad.

      Dr. H. Bonar.

EIGHTH DAY.

———

Want of Will.

"Ye will not come to Me, that ye might have life."—John 5:40.

Hosea 7:11

Hosea 4:17

Isaiah 64:7

Proverbs 1:30

Matthew 9:10

Deut. 18:6

1 John 5:12

Revelation 21:8

Romans 3:3, 4

Deut. 30:19
Jeremiah 21:8
Ezekiel 18:31

I T is almost certain that some whose eyes glance over these pages will be conscious that they do not very much care to come to Christ; for this is at once the commonest and the most fatal hindrance. You cannot honestly say that you *want* to come. You perhaps go as far as to say, with momentary seriousness, "I wish that I wished!" but no farther. In your inmost heart you would rather be "let alone," not considering that *that* is the most terribly certain beginning of doom. You are not perfectly comfortable, but you are not so uncomfortable as to feel inclined to make any effort. And as long as you can keep from thinking about it, you say you are "very happy." Now believe me, yours is a ten times worse and more dangerous state than if you were a condemned murderer, knowing his doom, realizing his sin, and *therefore* seeking the Saviour and coming to Him "with all the desire of his mind."

For so long as you are not willing, *i.e.,* not actually and actively willing to come (for that is the meaning of the original), of course you cannot come. And without coming to Jesus you cannot have life. And if you do not have life, there is nothing but death for you,—the second death with all its unknown terrors, into the realities of which any moment may plunge you. Your not believing this makes no difference to the fact. Your doubting it makes no difference to its certainty. I assert it on the authority of the Word of God. "I call heaven and earth to record this day against you, that I have set before you life and death. Therefore choose life." For in not willing life, you are willing death, and "why will ye die?"

Why? Is it not utterly unreasonable? Would any but a lunatic walk with mirth and fun over the thin crust which hides unknown depths of boiling lava? Would you enjoy a picnic in the midst of it? Yet this is less mad than what you are doing.

Then you will say, "I can't help it! I can't make myself care!" Exactly so; and just in this fact lies, not your excuse, but your one hope and help. You cannot make yourself care to flee from the wrath to come. You cannot rouse yourself to be willing to come to Christ for salvation. But One can. And you may and can ask for the Holy Spirit to make you willing. You can say, "O God, give me Thy Holy Spirit to make me willing to come, for Jesus Christ's sake." God makes no condition whatever as to giving this. The Blessed Spirit is promised most simply and unconditionally "to them that ask Him." *This* promise says nothing even about desiring or thirsting: it premises absolutely nothing, but comes to the lowest depths of sin-paralyzed will—it is only and simply, "*Ask.*"

Remember that one spirit or the other is now working in you. It is very awful to read of "the spirit that now worketh in the children of disobedience"; and what is more direct disobedience than not coming when Jesus calls? Therefore "ask," and ask at once, for the other spirit, the Holy Spirit, who can make you "willing in the day of His power,"—God the Holy Ghost, who "worketh in us to will."

Think of Jesus saying, "How often would I," "but ye would not." *He* is willing.

May He give you "one heart to do the commandment of the King!"

Come, Holy Spirit, heavenly Dove,
With all Thy quickening powers!
Come, shed abroad a Saviour's love,
And that shall kindle ours!

DR. WATTS.

Margin references:
Ezekiel 33:11
Matthew 3:7
Hosea 13:9
Luke 11:9–13
Ephesians 2:2
Psalm 110:3
Philippians 2:13
Luke 13:34
2 Chron. 30:12

NINTH DAY.

The Call of the Spirit.

"And the Spirit and the Bride say, Come."—Revelation 22:17.

Romans 15:30
Ps. 143:10, P.V.R.

Ephesians 4:30
Isaiah 63:10
Acts 7:51
2 Thess. 2:13
Hebrews 12:14

2 Timothy 3:16
2 Peter 1:21

John 14:26

Romans 2:4

2 Cor. 5:20

Eph. 5:25–32
2 Chron. 36:15, 16

HAVE you thought about "the love of the Spirit"? Have you realized that God's "loving Spirit" says to you, "Come"? Are you conscious that if you refuse to listen to this gentlest call, you are "grieving" the Holy Spirit of God,—"vexing" Him by the rebellion to which this refusal really amounts,—"resisting" the Holy Ghost, whose power alone can work in you the holiness without which you can never see the Lord?

Every "Come!" in the Bible is the call of the Spirit. For "all Scripture is given by inspiration of God," and the "holy men of God spake as they were moved by the Holy Ghost." And every time that a still small voice in your heart says "Come," it is the call of the Spirit. Every time the remembrance of the Saviour's sweetest spoken word floats across your mind, it is the Holy Spirit's fulfilment of our Lord's promise that "He shall bring all things to your remembrance, whatsoever I have said unto you." Last time those words, "Come unto Me," came into your mind, whether in some wakeful night hour, or suddenly and unaccountably amid the stir of the day, did you think that it was the very voice of the Holy Spirit speaking in your heart? Or did you let other voices drown it, not knowing that the goodness of God was leading you by it?

Every time an ambassador of Christ bids you come, and every time that any one who loves Him tries to speak a word for Jesus to you, it is the call of the Spirit and the Bride; for the Bride is the Church of Christ, and she is the privileged instrument through which the clear music of the call is oftenest heard.

What makes you take the trouble to read this book? Why is there any attraction at all for you in the subject? Is it not that the Holy Spirit is causing your heart to vibrate, it may be but very feebly as yet, at the thrill of His secret call? Your awakening wish to come is the echo of that call. If you stop and listen, it will be heard more distinctly and winningly. The call will grow fuller and stronger as you turn and yield, and follow it. And the same blessed Spirit will give you power to do this. He will show you your need of Jesus, and He will testify of Jesus to you, so that you shall be willing to come. Do you feel very helpless about it? Do you wish you had the mighty aid of the Almighty Spirit, so that you might rise and come while Jesus of Nazareth passeth by? Then why do you not ask for it? Who is to blame if you do not have what is to be had for the asking? Christ Himself has put the promise in the very plainest words: "Ask, and it shall be given you," and "Every one that asketh receiveth." What could you wish Him to say more? What could He possibly say more? Clearly, if you have not, it is because you ask not. But if you *are* asking for the Holy Spirit in the name of Jesus, you have already the earnest of the Spirit, and you shall have more and more. So take courage!

But it is no light thing to put away a holy desire, however feeble; because it sprang not from your own heart, but is the voice of the Spirit saying, Come! It will not always speak, if not obeyed. Turn back from Revelation to Genesis, and you find the shadow of the bright light of the winning call in the unchanged warning note: "My Spirit shall not always strive with man." Not *always,* dear, unknown friend whom I would fain win for my Lord,—not *always!* But He is striving now, He is calling now, "To-day, if ye will hear His voice." Listen, yield, come!

1 Thess. 5:24
John 15:26
John 5:7
Mark 10:47–49

Luke 11:13
Matthew 7:7, 8

James 4:2

2 Cor. 1:22
Matthew 13:12

Genesis 6:3
Proverbs 29:1

Hebrews 4:7

TENTH DAY.

Come and See.

"He (Jesus) saith unto them, Come and see." "Philip saith unto him, Come and see."—John 1:39, 46.

Jn 1:45; Heb 2:9

2 Cor. 5:14

Romans 10:1

Jeremiah 20:9

John 4:28, 29

John 4:26

1 Cor. 9:16

2 Samuel 24:24

Acts 19:9

Acts 9:2

Jeremiah 1:6

Acts 4:20

2 Cor. 4:13

1 John 1:3

Revelation 22:17

WHEN Jesus had found Philip, Philip *knew* that he had found Him. And the next thing to knowing that "we have found Him" is to find some one else, and say, "Come and see!" I say it now to you, dear friend, known or unknown, "We have found Him!" "We see Jesus!" If you only knew the irresistible longing, the very heart's desire that you should find and see Him too, you would pardon all the pertinacity, all the insistence, with which again and again we say, "Come and see!" The woman of Samaria left her water-pot, and went her way into the city with the same message: "Come, see a man which told me all that ever I did." And we to whom Jesus has said, "I that speak unto thee am He," cannot do otherwise or less.

It is not always very easy to say it. You little know how much it sometimes costs us! You do not know that though the few words seem so easily spoken, and you take them as a matter of course from us, because you know we are of "that way" of thinking, they may have cost us not a little wrestling with God for faith and courage to utter them, and an effort which will leave us weary and exhausted. But "we cannot but speak the things which we have seen and heard"; "we also believe, and *therefore* speak." We have seen Jesus, and therefore we must tell you of the sight, and entreat you to "Come and see." Understand or misunderstand us as you will, we must "say, Come!"

But what is it that we are so burningly eager for you to see? Very likely you suppose it is just that we have a certain set of views that we have taken up, and we want you to hold the same. You think it is merely that we want to bring you over to our opinions, and that we want to have the satisfaction of getting you to agree with us! Oh, how wide of the mark! It is no such thing. We are not speaking of what we think, but "we speak that we do know, and testify that we have seen." We have seen by faith the only sight that is worth gazing upon, the sight that satisfies the angels, the sight that is enough for the joy and satisfaction of immortal vision throughout eternity. One thing we know, that, whereas we were blind, now we see.

We see Jesus, as our Lord and our God.

We see Him as the very Saviour we need, and the very Friend we craved.

We see Him as "the Son of God, who loved me and gave Himself for me."

We see Him wounded for our transgressions, and bruised for our iniquities; our Substitute and our Sin-bearer.

We see Him, too, crowned with glory and honour, and we rejoice in His glory and beauty; we make our boast of Him.

If you say to us, "What is thy Beloved more than another beloved?" we reply, "My beloved is the chiefest among ten thousand. Yea, He is altogether lovely."

It is not at all only for your own sakes that we want you so very much to come and see. We do want you to look and be saved. But our earnestness has a stronger spring than even that. We love our Lord, so that we cannot bear Him not to be esteemed aright. We cannot bear Him to be thought little of, and to be misunderstood; it is pain, real pain, to us when He is not appreciated and loved and adored,—when all that He has done is treated as not worth whole-hearted gratitude and love,—when His great and blood-bought salvation is neglected. For His own beloved sake, for His own glory's sake, we want you to come and see, that you may love and bless and glorify Him!

But, remember, this is not only our feeble human entreaty; it is Jesus Himself who first said, and still says, "Come and see!" *He* says, "Behold Me, behold Me!"

I know what you will say when you have come. You will

Margin references:

1 John 4:14
John 3:11
Hebrews 11:27
1 Timothy 3:16

John 9:25

John 20:28

Galatians 2:20

Isaiah 53:5

Hebrews 2:9
2 Cor. 3:18; Zech. 9:17; Psalm 34:2
Song. 5:9,10,16

Psalm 45:2

Isaiah 45:22

John 1:5, 11
1 Peter 2:4
Isaiah 53:3

Lament. 1:12

Hebrews 2:3

Isaiah 65:1

1 Kings 10:7

2 Chron. 9:6

say, "Howbeit I believed not their words *until* I came, and mine eyes had seen it: and, behold, the half was not told me. Thou exceedest the fame that I heard!"

> O Master, blessèd Master, it is hard indeed to know
> That thousands round our daily path misunder-
>   stand Thee so!
> Despisèd and rejected yet, no beauty they can see,
> O King of glory and of grace, belovèd Lord, in
>   Thee.
>
> O Saviour, precious Saviour, come in all Thy power
>   and grace,
> And take away the veil that hides the glory of Thy
>   face!
> Oh, manifest the marvels of Thy tenderness and
>   love,
> And let thy name be blessed and praised all other
>   names above!

ELEVENTH DAY.

The Safe Venture.

"Bid me come unto Thee … And He said, Come."—Matthew 14:28, 29.

Psalm 107:14

Job 16:16

Romans 7:13

Jeremiah 17:9

Matthew 14:25

Matthew 14:27

Job 23:15–17

Matthew 14:26

IF Jesus says, "Come!" don't you think you may venture? Perhaps it is night in your soul,—as dark as ever it can be. It would not be so bad if you could even distinctly see the waves of the troubled sea on which you are tossing. You do not know where you are. All seems vague and uncertain and wretched and confused. And though the Lord Jesus is very near you, though He has come to you walking on the water, and has said, "It is I, be not afraid," you cannot see Him, and you are not at all sure it is His voice; or if it is, that He is speaking to you. So of course you are "troubled."

And if, in this trouble, you go on trying to steer and row for yourself, these same waves will prove themselves to be awful realities, and you will be lost in the storm. Do not venture that; but venture out through the darkness and upon the waves at the bare word of Jesus.

Matthew 11:28

You do not need even to say, "Lord, bid me come to Thee!" for He has done that already. Jesus *has* bid you "Come!" and the bidding would be no more real if He opened the heavens, and said it again to you from the right hand of the throne of God. So the only question is, Will you venture?

Matthew 24:35

John 12:48

Numbers 23:19

Matthew 8:8

Revelation 7:9

True, it is but a word, but think Whose word! Could the word that Jesus Christ Himself uttered be a vain deceit? Is not the Person the guarantee of the word? "The word only," of the Son of God has proved enough for every one of the great multitude that no man could number, and it will be enough for you.

Isaiah 50:10

It does not matter in the least that you cannot see, and that you cannot feel, and that you cannot hear or distinguish anything else at all. It does not matter in the least

Isaiah 9:5
2 Chron. 20:12

John 6:21

Isaiah 57:20
2 Peter 1:9
Hebrews 12:1
2 Timothy 2:13

Matthew 14:24

Mark 5:33

Matthew 14:30

Matthew 14:31
Esther 4:16
John 10:27, 28
John 6:37
Jeremiah 16:21
Zephaniah 3:17

Isaiah 52:6

that you feel miserable and confused, and that you don't know what will come next. It does not matter in the least that you cannot exactly understand how this simple coming can result in calm, and peace, and safety, and finding yourself at the land. It does not matter in the least that the waters are casting up all the mire and dirt of all the sinfulness of heart and life, the "old sins," and the besetting sins. It does not matter in the least that all the winds of doubt seem let loose upon you, boisterous and blowing from every point to which you turn. All this, and everything else that is "contrary," is only so much the more reason for the simple venture. Just only you "come!" And even if in the very act of coming you are afraid, and think you are beginning to sink, come on with the cry, "Lord, save me!" and immediately Jesus will save you, and with the strong grasp of His hand the unanswerable question will come, "Wherefore didst thou doubt?" You need not say, "If I perish, I perish," for you will not perish, and cannot perish, in this blessed venture of your soul upon His word. He "will cause you to know His hand and His might"; "He will save, He will rejoice over thee with joy; *He* will rest in His love," and *you* shall rest in His love, now and for ever.

"They shall know in that day that I am He that doth speak; behold, it is I."

> Come, ye weary, heavy laden,
> Lost and ruined by the fall;
> If you tarry till you're better,
> You will never come at all.
> Not the righteous,
> Sinners Jesus came to call.
>
> Lo! the incarnate God, ascended,
> Pleads the merit of His blood;
> Venture on Him, venture wholly,
> Let no other trust intrude.
> None but Jesus
> Can do helpless sinners good.

JOSEPH HART.

TWELFTH DAY.

Coming Boldly.

" Let us therefore come boldly unto the throne of grace, that we may obtain mercy, and find grace to help in time of need."—Hebrews 4:16.

Hebrews 7:26
Hebrews 4:14, 15

Zechariah 6:13
Hebrews 7:25
Hebrews 4:16

Revelation 21:8
Isaiah 7:9

Matthew 8:26

Ephesians 2:8
John 4:10
Ezekiel 36:37
James 1:5

Matthew 7:7
James 4:2

Luke 17:5
Ephesians 3:11,12

" THEREFORE ! " because we have " such an High Priest," touched with the feeling of our infirmities, and in all points tempted like as we are; because He is " a Priest upon His throne," ever living, with His royal power to save to the uttermost, and His priestly power to make intercession: " let us *therefore* come boldly unto the throne of grace."

Boldness and faith go together; fear and unbelief go together. " If ye will not believe, surely ye shall not be established." It is always want of faith that is at the bottom of all fear. "Why are ye fearful?" is the question for those " of little faith." So, in order to come boldly, and therefore joyfully, all we need is more faith in the Great High Priest who sits upon the throne of grace.

Now, do not sigh, "Ah, I wish I had more faith!" It will not come to you by languid lamentations about your want of faith. "It is the gift of God." And if thou knewest this gift of God, and who it is that only waits to be inquired of, that He may give it thee, surely thou wouldst ask of Him! For He giveth to all men liberally, and upbraideth not,—not even with all your neglect of Him and His gifts. Just *ask!* and He says, "It shall be given you." "Ye have not, because ye ask not." And let the least glimmer of dawning faith in your heart lead you to go on asking, and to pray continually, "Lord, increase our faith." Then you will be able to come boldly; for "in Christ Jesus our Lord ... we have boldness and access with confidence by the faith of Him."

People do not come for what they do not want. Until the Holy Spirit shows us our need of mercy, and puts reality into

Psalm 51:1

the Litany prayer, "Have mercy upon us miserable sinners," we shall never come to the throne of grace to obtain mercy.

> "He that into God's kingdom comes,
> Must enter by this door."

Luke 18:13

So, if you have never yet felt that you could sincerely say, "God be merciful to *me* a sinner" (or, as the Greek has it more emphatically, "to me, *the* sinner"), and therefore have never yet felt particularly anxious to come to the throne of grace to obtain it, I would urgently entreat you to pray, "Lord, show me myself!" When the Holy Spirit answers that prayer, you will be eager enough to come and obtain

Luke 10:42

mercy! It will be the one thing then that you will be particularly anxious about.

Obtaining mercy comes first; *then* finding grace to help in time of need. You cannot reverse God's order. You will not find grace to help in time of need till you have sought and found mercy to save. You have no right to reckon on God's help and protection and guidance, and all the other

Galatians 3:26

splendid privileges which He promises to "the children of God by faith in Jesus Christ," until you have this first blessing, the mercy of God in Christ Jesus; for it is "in" Jesus

2 Cor. 1:19, 20

Christ that all the promises of God are yea, and Amen. But

Eph. 2:4; Micah 7:18

He is "rich in mercy," and "delighteth in mercy." All who have come to the throne of grace for it, "are now the peo-

1 Peter 2:10

ple of God, which had not obtained mercy, but now have obtained mercy." And then no less surely will they, and do

Hebrews 4:16

they, "find grace to help in every time of need."

"Let *us* therefore come boldly!"

> Behold the throne of grace!
> The promise calls me near;
> There Jesus shows a smiling face,
> And waits to answer prayer.
>
> My soul, ask what thou wilt,
> Thou canst not be too bold:
> Since His own blood for thee He spilt,
> What else can He withhold?
>
> JOHN NEWTON.

THIRTEENTH DAY.

A Hindrance.

"First be reconciled to thy brother, and then come and offer thy gift."—Matthew 5:24.

Proverbs 23:26
Jeremiah 17:9
Matthew 15:19

I T is a strange gift that we have to bring,—so strange, that it is in one sense "nothing," and yet in another sense everything. He asks us for it, saying, "Give Me thine heart"; and this heart of ours, this gift that we are to bring, worthless and yet priceless, is one mass of sins and burdens. Jesus asks for it just as it is, with all the sins and all the burdens; and the moment it is given over to Him, the sins are cleansed and the burdens are borne for us.

Job 15:11
Hosea 10:2

Do you wish to come to Him with it, and yet find that there seems something preventing you from really doing so? If so, the verse at the head of this chapter may throw God's light upon the secret obstacle. "Is there any secret thing with *thee?*" Christ will either accept the gift altogether, or not at all. If there is something which you do not really mean to do right about,—some sin which you have no real intention of giving up,—it will be a fatal barrier. He for-

1 John 1:7

1 Cor. 15:17
1 Cor. 3:3
Acts 8:21

gives all or none. If you are but willing, His precious blood shall cleanse you from *all* sin. But He does not save by halves; and if there is a sin knowingly kept back, then "ye are yet in your sins," and "thou hast neither part nor lot in this matter; *for* thy heart is not right in the sight of God."

This may seem a very stern way of putting it; but when such tremendous issues hang upon it, is it not folly to shrink from looking the matter straight in the face? The Lord says, "First be reconciled to thy brother, and *then* come and offer thy gift."

James 5:16

This may be literally your case. Some one may have somewhat against you,—an old quarrel, or a fresh misunderstanding,—and you are too proud to acknowledge your fault, or your share of it; or you are too timid, or even too idle to do so. When there are faults on both sides, it is pretty often the one most in fault who is the least ready to forgive. Now do look into the matter, and see if you are truly "in love and charity with all men." It is no use trying to explain away your daily words, "Forgive us our trespasses, as we forgive them that trespass against us," for Christ Himself has explained and emphasized them. He said, "But if ye forgive not men their trespasses, neither will your Father forgive your trespasses." There is no evading this. There is absolutely *no* forgiveness for you, if you do not forgive; for "who can forgive sins but God only?"

And it is no use saying, "Well, I will forgive, but I can't forget!" You know quite well in your heart that the very tone in which you say that, shows that you are not really forgiving, and God knows what is at the bottom of your "can't *forget!*"

Don't turn round fiercely, and say, "But if I can't, I can't!" For "the things which are impossible with men, are possible with God."

Read the 45th of Genesis, and see how Joseph forgave; and remember that the same Spirit of God which was in him is freely promised to you for the asking.

And then look at the still greater example of perfect forgiveness,—hear the smitten King in His lonely death-agony saying, "Father, forgive them!" "For He knew that forgiveness would raise them to the very level of His throne; so He must have literally loved His murderers with the love wherewith His Father loved Him." Oh, it is not hard to forgive anything, when one looks away to the forgiveness of Jesus.

Then come and offer thy gift.

Heb. 12:14, 15
1 John 3:10, 15

Matthew 6:15

Mark 2:7
Compare
Hebrews 8:12

Revelation 2:23
John 2:25

Luke 18:27

Genesis 45:1–15

Genesis 41:38

Luke 23:34

John 17:26
Ephesians 4:32

FOURTEENTH DAY.

The Entreaty to Come.

"Come near to me, I *pray* you."—Genesis 45:4.

Genesis 45:1,2

"THERE stood no man with him, while Joseph made himself known to his brethren. And he wept aloud." They had hated him, conspired against him to slay him, very nearly killed him, sold him into exile and slavery, and here was the brother's recompense for all this—love! No such exquisite story of love and forgiveness was ever imagined by any writer; no such climax of tenderness as Joseph's words through his tears, "Come near to me, I pray you." Only one thing surpasses the type, and that is the antitype.

Isaiah 53:12
Zechariah 13:6
Isaiah 53:5
1 Cor. 15:3

Psalm 116:12
2 Cor. 5:15
1 Peter 3:18
Philippians 3:8

Our Elder Brother was more than "very nearly killed." He poured out His soul unto death. We are not innocent of His blood; for "He was wounded for *our* transgressions, He was bruised for *our* iniquities." "Christ died *for our sins*." Mark that,—not merely "for us," but "*for our sins*," for *yours*. And where has been the love and gratitude that you have owed Him all this time? Where has been the mere acknowledgment of what He has suffered for your sins? He did this for you, and because of you. And what have you done for Him, and because of Him?

Jeremiah 29:11

And what could you now expect from Him? What did Joseph's brothers expect after their behaviour to him? Well may the Lord say, "I know the thoughts that I think towards you—thoughts of peace, and not of evil." For just as Joseph's words to his brethren were not, "Go away, I will have no more to do with you," so the Lord Jesus "upbraideth not," but says, "Come near to Me, I *pray* you."

His whole life says it. It is the epitome of all He said and did,—winning, beseeching, entreating the far-off to

Ephesians 2:13

come nigh, giving His own blood that they might be made nigh.

Zechariah 13:6

What is the eloquence of "those wounds in Thine hands"? Are they not always saying, "I *pray* you"? For "all

Romans 10:21

day long I have stretched forth My hands unto a disobedient and gainsaying people."

"All day long," while you are dressing, and eating, and talking, and laughing, and working or amusing yourself, Jesus is stretching forth His hands to you, calling you, waiting for you, looking for the first little thrill of recognition from

Acts 9:5

you, saying, "I am Jesus whom thou persecutest, whom thou neglectest, whom thou grievest."

Genesis 45:3
Job 23:15
Psalm 139:7

Joseph's brethren were troubled at his presence. Do *you* reply, "Therefore I am troubled at His presence; when I consider, I am afraid of Him"? Would you, honestly, rather flee from His presence? Stay and listen.

"Come near to Me, I pray you."

Psalm 130:4
1 Peter 2:24

There is forgiveness with Him; will you not come and receive it?—Forgiveness for you, though every sin of yours that is forgiven had to be borne in His dying agony. His love

Luke 23:34

has not changed from the moment when He said, "Father, forgive them." What must that love have been! And what must it be for you and me, for whom He cannot make the gracious excuse, "They know not what they do!"

Genesis 45:1

Come *alone* to Him, and Jesus will make known Himself and His forgiving love to you.

> One there is above all others,
>   Well deserves the name of Friend;
> His is love beyond a brother's,
>   Costly, free, and knows no end:
> They who once His kindness prove
> Find it everlasting love.

JOHN NEWTON.

FIFTEENTH DAY.

_____

The Command to Come.

"Come unto me ... Now thou art commanded, this do ye, ... and come."
—Genesis 45:18, 19.

Matthew 22:2, 3

W E are too much inclined to forget that "Come" is not merely an invitation, but a command. An ordinary invitation can be accepted or refused but a Royal Invitation is always a Royal Command, giving no option, but requiring obedience. Therefore, just so long as we are hanging back, just so long as we have not come to Jesus, we are living in a state of actual disobedience to Him.

Joseph, whose dealings with his brethren are among the most beautiful types, was to say to them not only, "Come unto me," but "Now thou art *commanded,* this do ye,—and come!"

Matthew 11:28

Deut. 30:11, 14

The Lord Jesus, the King of Glory, has said the very same words, "Come unto Me!" to you and me. And so we *are* commanded. There is no excusing ourselves by any uncertainty about it. The very moment that "Come" first fell on our heart, the command was upon us, and we were responsible for obeying it. And every moment since, we have been disobeying the plainest and sweetest word of command that ever fell on mortal ear, unless we have really and truly "come to Jesus."

So it is not at all a light thing, but a heavy and tremendous sin in which we are living,—the sin of direct and continued disobedience to Christ.

Genesis 3:24

Romans 5:19

Proverbs 1:24–26

Heb. 10:28, 29

If one *single* and *sudden* act of disobedience was enough to lose Paradise and lead to incalculable consequences of misery, what about this persistence in refusal to obey this strong and gentle command, clearly understood, continually reiterated, and unmistakeably personal, Christ's personal command to you personally? "Death without mercy" is as terrible a punishment as can well be imagined; but what must be the "much sorer punishment" than *that*, which is denounced by the Word of our God on those who, instead of merely "despising Moses' law," have "trodden under foot the Son of God"?

Acts 1:11

We must not and dare not leave out of sight, the awful revelation that it is the Lord Jesus Himself, the very same tender Saviour who now bids you "Come," who will take

2 Thess. 1:7–9
Matt. 25:41, 46

vengeance in flaming fire on them "that obey not the gospel of our Lord Jesus Christ, who shall be punished with everlasting destruction from the presence of the Lord."

When I began to write this little book, I never meant to say all this. I only wanted to win you by the sweet, sweet

Romans 10:21
Luke 13:8
Romans 2:4

music of my Master's call. I only meant to tell you of His patient, forbearing love, waiting so long for you, wanting you to come to Him. But what can I do? Half a truth is not "the truth." You may not like it; but I dare not speak to you

Isaiah 30:10
Acts 20:27
Numbers 22:18

only smooth things, I dare not shun to declare unto you the whole counsel of God in this matter. "I cannot go beyond the word of the Lord my God to do *less*." I should come un-

Revelation 22:19

der the awful condemnation of those who "take away from the words of the book," if I did not tell the whole message.

Jeremiah 26:2

The Lord has said, "Diminish not a word," and so I entreat you to look for yourselves at the passages I have quoted, and "*hear* the word of the Lord" in them.

Hebrews 12:25

Oh, "see that ye refuse not Him that speaketh!" If you do not obey the "Come unto Me," there remaineth nothing

Matthew 25:41

for you but the "Depart from Me."

Life alone is found in Jesus
Only there 'tis offered thee,—
Offered without price or money,
'Tis the gift of God sent free:
Take salvation,
Take it now, and happy be!

ALBERT MIDLANE.

SIXTEENTH DAY.

Royal Largesse.

"Come unto Me: and I will give you the good of the land of Egypt, and ye shall eat the fat of the land … Also regard not your stuff: for the good of all the land of Egypt is yours."—Genesis 45:18, 20.

Matthew 19:22

"IF I become a Christian, I shall have to give up so many things!" Spoken or unspoken, this is the invariable thought of every one who has not found Christ. The presence of this thought is an actual test as to whether you have come to Him or not; for the moment you have really come, you will know better!

Philippians 3:7

"Giving up" this, that, and the other, is a downright *unfair* way of putting it; unless, indeed, the magnificent gain is distinctly set against the paltry loss. As well talk of an oak tree "giving up" the withered leaves which have clung to the dry twigs all the winter, when the sap begins to rise fresh and strong, and the promise of all the splendour of summer foliage is near!

Genesis 45:11
Genesis 47:11, 27

The sons of Jacob were called away from their famine-stricken fields by their brother, that they might be "nourished" by him, and share his prosperity, and dwell "in the best of the land"; receiving from his hand a place and possessions far beyond what they had "given up." Of course they could not have all this till they had actually come to him! Before they came, they had only his bare word for it.

Genesis 46:31
Genesis 47:11, 12

But they considered his word enough, and they came; and he kept his word to the full.

2 Cor. 9:15

Not less, but infinitely more, does the Lord Jesus, our Lord and Brother, hold forth to you. Is His word worthy of less belief? Over and above the unspeakable gift of eternal life, He promises to those who leave anything for His sake

Mark 10:30 that they "shall receive an hundred-fold *now, in this time!*" Do you suppose He did not mean what He said?

Listen again to the twin promises, negative and positive, in their all-inclusive simplicity: "No good thing will He Psalm 84:11 withhold from them that walk uprightly"; and "The Lord Psalm 85:12 will give that which is good." And yet your secret feeling is, Matthew 7:11 that if you come and give yourself up to Him, you will have to go without all sorts of things that you fancy are good and Psalm 34:10 nice and pleasant, and that you will find yourself let in for all sorts of things which do not seem to you "good" at all! Is this fair, when He has said positively just the opposite?

Listen again to what He says to those who *have* come, and who are His own: "Whether ... the world, or life, or 1 Cor. 3:22 death, or things present, or things to come; *all are yours!*" Job 36:11 What do you make of that? It is not figurative, but perfectly true and literal. Only you will never be able to understand 1 Cor. 2:14 it, until the next verse is true of you: "Ye are Christ's." *Then* 1 Cor. 3:23 another verse will be true of you: "Now we have received, 1 Cor. 2:12 not the spirit of the world, but the Spirit which is of God; that we might *know* the things which are freely given to us Luke 11:13 of God." Ask for that blessed Spirit of God, and you will receive it, and *then* you will understand.

Proverbs 28:5 Knowing what he was purposing to do for them as soon as they came, Joseph naturally said to his brethren, "Also re- Genesis 45:20 gard not your stuff; for the good of all the land of Egypt is yours." Take this advice, "regard not your stuff!" Howev- er much you have or may have to give up for Christ, oh, *do* 2 Chron. 25:9 believe the words of His prophet: "The Lord is able to give thee *much more* than this!"

Can you not instinctively feel what a thrill of deep Philippians 3:8 triumphant joy there is in St. Paul's words: "Yea, doubt- less, and I count all things but loss for the excellency of the knowledge of Christ Jesus my Lord!" Did you ever feel any- thing like as glad as that? Christ Jesus my Lord is willing and waiting to give that same fulness of gladness and bless- ing to every one who will take Him at His word and come to Him.

Yes, to *you!*

Oh, the happiness arising
   From the life of grace within,
When the soul is realizing
   Conquests over hell and sin!
     Happy moments!
   Heavenly joys on earth begin.

On the Saviour's fulness living,
   All His saints obtain delight;
With the strength which He is giving,
   They can wrestle, they can fight.
     Happy moments,
   When King Jesus is in sight!

JOSEPH IRONS.

SEVENTEENTH DAY.

Tarry Not.

"Come down unto me, tarry not."—Genesis 45:9

Genesis 43:1, 2

IT is just this "tarrying" that is hindering so many from coming to the Saviour. What reason could there be for Joseph's brethren to "tarry," and go on starving a little longer in their own land, when Joseph was waiting to settle them and their father and their whole families in the land

Genesis 47:11

of Goshen "in the best of the land"? And what reason can there be for you to tarry, and go on starved and unsatisfied a little longer, when the Lord Jesus is waiting to receive you

Psalm 106:24
Luke 15:13, 16

into the "pleasant land" of His all-satisfying love? Why tarry in the "far country" with the husks and the heart-loneliness? "Ye shall haste!" said Joseph, for his heart was eager to do great things for them.

Romans 2:4

If you grant the reality of Christ's love at all, do you not see that delay in coming down to Him, and hesitation in letting Him save you in His own way (and there is no oth-

Song. 5:2, 6

er), and putting Him off from day to day, must be wounding His love?

Jeremiah 13:21

Why *do* you tarry? Have you any reason whatever to give Him? "What wilt thou say?" Do not flatter yourself that all this delay and putting off is any preparation for coming, much less any part of coming to Him. There are no steps in coming to Jesus. Either you come, or you do not come. There is only the "one step, out of self, into Christ." There are no gradations of approach marked out in His Word. If you think there are, search and see; do not

Acts 17:11, 12

take my word for it; look for yourself, and see what is the Lord's word about it.

You have nothing to gain, but very much, perhaps everything, to lose by "tarrying." You are accumulating the

Acts 24:25

guilt of disobedience. You are, it may be very unconsciously,

Hebrews 3:7, 8

hardening your heart, and making the great step more and more difficult. Instead of being in a better position for coming tomorrow, you will be in a worse one.

While you are doing nothing, the enemy is very busy strengthening his toils around you, and they will be stronger to-morrow than to-day.

While you are, as you fancy, only lying still, you are drifting fast down the stream into the stronger current, nearing the rapids, nearing the fatal fall.

Genesis 19:17

It is a question of life and death. "Escape for thy life; look not behind thee, neither stay thou in all the plain." It is the old story of

"If you tarry till you're better,
You will never come at all."

I do not know any one promise in all the Bible for the lingerers. And if you put yourself out of the sphere of God's promises, what have you to found any hope at all upon?

Hebrews 4:7

"Tarry not!" Oh, if I could but reach you and rouse you!

"And if I care
For one unknown, oh how much more doth He!"

2 Peter 3:9

Matthew 22:3, 5

For one who perishes through straightforward refusal, there are probably thousands who perish through *putting off.*

Hebrews 12:25
Hebrews 2:3

"How shall we escape if we" *refuse*—no, if we merely "*neglect*—so great salvation?"

Yet there is room! The Lamb's bright hall of song,
With its fair glory, beckons thee along.

Yet there is room! Still open stands the gate,
The gate of love; it is not yet too late.

Pass in, pass in! That banquet is for thee;
That cup of everlasting love is free.

Ere night that gate might close, and seal thy doom;
Then the last, low, long cry,—"No room, no room!"

DR. H. BONAR.

EIGHTEENTH DAY.

Without Christ.

"At that time ye were without Christ."—Ephesians 2:12.

John 6:68
Luke 19:10
1 Peter 1:18, 19
Revelation 5:9
Romans 3:22
Ephesians 1:7
Hebrews 6:19
Galatians 6:14

I COULD not do without Thee,
  O Saviour of the lost!
Whose precious blood redeemed me,
  At such tremendous cost.
Thy righteousness, Thy pardon,
  Thy precious blood—must be
My only hope and comfort,
  My glory and my plea.

Psalm 73:23
Song. 5:10
Philippians 3:8
Matthew 13:44
1 Peter 2:7
Psalm 18:2
Psalm 34:8
John 1:46

I could not do without Him!
  Jesus is more to me
Than all the richest, fairest gifts
  Of earth could ever be.
But the more I find Him precious,
  And the more I find Him true,
The more I long for you to find
  What He can be to you.

Hosea 13:9
Matthew 20:30
Isaiah 30:18
Isaiah 30:19
2 Cor. 6:17
Isaiah 43:1
Hosea 11:8
Hosea 14:2

You need not do without Him,
  For He is passing by;
He is waiting to be gracious,
  Only waiting for your cry.
He is waiting to receive you,—
  To make you all His own!
Why will you do without Him,
  And wander on alone?

Hosea 13:10
Titus 3:4
Romans 5:8
John 4:14

Why will you do without Him?
  Is He not kind indeed?
Did He not die to save you?
  Is He not all you need?

Acts 5:31
John 15:14
Hosea 2:20
John 13:1

Do you not want a Saviour?
    Do you not want a Friend?
One who will love you faithfully,
    And love you to the end?

Jeremiah 4:30
Matthew 24:35
1 John 2:17
Psalm 144:4
James 4:14
Proverbs 27:1
Proverbs 29:1
Isaiah 33:14

Why will you do without Him?
    The Word of God is true;
The world is passing to its doom,
    And you are passing too.
It may be, no to-morrow
    Shall dawn for you or me;
Why will you run the awful risk
    Of all eternity?

Hosea 9:5
Eccles. 12:1
Isaiah 59:9, 10
Hosea 2:6
Hosea 13:9,10
Jeremiah 2:17
Jeremiah 2:25
Job 7:4

What will you do without Him
    In the long and dreary day
Of trouble and perplexity,
    When you do not know the way;
And no one else can help you,
    And no one guides you right,
And hope comes not with morning,
    And rest comes not with night?

Romans 7:24
John 8:33,34
2 Peter 2:19
Romans 8:2
Psalm 38:4
Ezekiel 33:10
Jeremiah 17:9
Jeremiah 17:14

You could not do without Him,
    If once He made you see
The fetters that enchain you
    Till He hath set you free;
If once you saw the fearful load
    Of sin upon your soul,—
The hidden plague that ends in death,
    Unless He makes you whole!

Jeremiah 12:5
Eccles. 12:3
Song. 8:6, 7
1 John 4:18
Jeremiah 13:16
Job 8:13, 14
Job 10:21,22
Psalm 23:4

What will you do without Him
    When death is drawing near,
Without His love—the only love
    That casts out every fear;
When the shadow-valley opens,
    Unlighted and unknown,
And the terrors of its darkness
    Must all be passed alone?

Revelation 6:17	What will you do without Him
Revelation 20:11	When the great White Throne is set,
Romans 2:16	And the Judge who never can mistake,
Hosea 7:2	And never can forget,—
2 Cor. 5:10	The Judge, whom you have never here
Matthew 7:23	As Friend and Saviour sought,
Romans 14:12	Shall summon you to give account
Matthew 12:36	Of deed, and word, and thought?

Revelation 6:17 | What will you do without Him
Revelation 20:11 | When the great White Throne is set,
Romans 2:16 | And the Judge who never can mistake,
Hosea 7:2 | And never can forget,—
2 Cor. 5:10 | The Judge, whom you have never here
Matthew 7:23 | As Friend and Saviour sought,
Romans 14:12 | Shall summon you to give account
Matthew 12:36 | Of deed, and word, and thought?

Matthew 25:11 | What will you do without Him
Revelation 3:7 | When He hath shut the door,
Hebrews 3:19 | And you are left outside, because
John 5:40 | You would not come before;
Luke 13:25 | When it is no use knocking,
Hebrews 12:17 | No use to stand and wait,
Revelation 22:11 | For the word of doom tolls through your heart,
Luke 16:26 | That terrible "Too late"?

John 14:6 | You cannot do without Him!
1 Timothy 2:5 | There is no other name
Acts 4:12 | By which you ever *can* be saved,—
Ephesians 2:12 | No way, no hope, no claim!
Mark 8:36 | Without Him—everlasting loss
John 3:36 | Of love, and life, and light!
Matthew 25:41 | Without Him—everlasting woe,
Matthew 8:12 | And everlasting night.

Song. 4:8 | But with Him—oh! *with Jesus!*—
John 17:24 | Are any words so blest?
Isaiah 35:10 | With Jesus—everlasting joy
1 Thess. 4:17 | And everlasting rest!
Psalm 107:9 | With Jesus—all the empty heart
Ephesians 3:19,20 | Filled with His perfect love!
Isaiah 26:3 | With Jesus—perfect peace below,
Psalm 16:11 | And perfect bliss above!

Jeremiah 5:31 | Why should you do without Him?—
Revelation 3:20 | It is not yet too late;
2 Cor. 6:2 | He has not closed the day of grace,
Matthew 7:13 | He has not shut the gate.

Mark 10:49	He calls you—hush! He calls you!—
John 6:67	He would not have you go
Hosea 2:14	Another step without Him,
John 15:13	Because He loves you so.
Ezekiel 33:11	Why will you do without Him?
John 7:37	He calls and calls again—
Matthew 11:28	"Come unto Me! Come unto Me!"
Isaiah 65:1, 2	Oh, shall He call in vain?
Matthew 23:37	He wants to have you with Him;
Psalm 13:1, 2	Do you not want Him too?
1 John 5:12	You cannot do without Him,
Jeremiah 31:3	And He wants—even you!

NINETEENTH DAY.

Come Away.

"My beloved spake, and said unto me, Rise up, my love, my fair one, and come away."—Song of Solomon 2:10.

WHAT a loving call! What astonishing condescension, that the Heavenly Bridegroom should use such words to—whom? Would you not like to be able to fill up that blank, and say, "My beloved spake, and said unto *me!*"

Perhaps you think this is too much for *you*. You feel too sinful and unworthy to be so loved,—too defiled to be called "my fair one." If so, will you turn to a wonderful picture of those upon whom He sets His love, and of what His love does for them, asking the Holy Spirit to open your eyes while you read it, that you may behold wondrous things out of it.

Ezekiel 16:5–14

Psalm 119:18

I will not quote it here, because I want you to go to His own Book for it. See in it how the Lord Jesus goes down to the very depths, and begins at the very beginning. Your case is not deeper than those depths; for it is even when we are *dead* in sins that the great love wherewith God loved us reaches and raises us. He says, "Awake, thou that sleepest, and rise *from the dead,* and Christ shall give thee light." You cannot be worse than "dead"; and the very sense of sin and death working in you is a proof that He has said unto you, "Live!"

Psalm 40:2

Eph. 2:1, 4, 5
Ephesians 5:14

Romans 7:13

Ezekiel 16:6

The call to arise and come away is a proof that He is passing by. And when Jesus passes by, He looks upon you, though you are not yet able to see Him. And He says that when He does this, it is "the time of love." And oh, what *that* implies! What will He not do, when the bright, warm,

Luke 18:37

Ezekiel 16:8

Ephesians 3:19	powerful rays of the love which passeth knowledge are fo-
John 17:26	cussed upon you, and He says even to you, "My love!" giv-
Song. 2:16	ing you the glorious right to respond, "My Beloved!"
Ezekiel 16:9	Read on, and see what He will do "then!" "*Then*" the
Psalm 51:2	"throughly" washing and the anointing which prepares you
Esther 2:12–14	for the delight of the King. "Then" the clothing, the gird-
Isaiah 61:10	ing and the covering, each with their treasures of signifi-
Psalm 45:13	cance. Then "also" the decking and the crowning, and the
Ezekiel 16:13, 14	being made "exceeding beautiful" and "perfect through My
	comeliness which I had put upon thee, saith the Lord God!"
Psalm 90:17	When He puts the beauty of the Lord our God upon us,
Song. 4:7	then He can indeed say, "My fair one!" "Fair" *only* with
Romans 8:7	His comeliness; otherwise the fairest natural character that
Song. 1:5	was ever seen is "black as the tents of Kedar,"—those mis-
	erable goats' hair tents, which are to this day the very type
	of the filthiest blackness. Yet with it, whatever your natural
	character, and whatever your added deformity through hav-
Jeremiah 13:23	ing been "accustomed to do evil," you will be "comely as
	the curtains of Solomon,"—the type of all that is costly and
	beautiful in colours and workmanship.
Philippians 2:13	*Let* Him do all this for you! Rise up and come away
	from all that pollutes and separates you from Him. "Shake
Isaiah 52:2; 60:1	thyself from the dust, and arise!" "Arise, shine, for thy
Psalm 68:13	Light is come!" "Though ye have lien among the pots, yet"
	(when you come to the Light that is come so close to you),
	"yet shall ye be as the wings of a dove covered with silver,
	and her feathers with yellow gold," shining and gleaming as
Malachi 4:2	you rise and come away, resplendent in the beams of the Sun
Mark 10:49	of righteousness. "Rise, He calleth thee!" "Come away!"

TWENTIETH DAY.

Coming After Jesus.

"Come and follow Me."—Matthew 19:21.

Ezekiel 33:31

1 Kings 18:21

FOLLOWING is the only proof of coming.

There is hardly a commoner lamentation than this: "I do not know whether I have come or not!" And nobody ever says that with a happy smile. It is always with a dismal look; and no wonder! When so much hinges upon it,—poverty or riches, safety or danger, life or death,—uncertainty must and will be miserable. Now, do you really want to know whether you have come or not? Our Lord gives you the test, "Come *and follow* Me!"

John 10:27; Matt. 20:34

If you are willing for that, willing with the will that issues in act and deed, then the coming is real.

Matthew 19:22

If you are not willing to follow, then you may dismiss at once any idea that perhaps you have come or are coming: there is no reality in it, and there is nothing for you but to go away sorrowful, as the rich young man did, who "came," but would not "follow."

Isaiah 28:17

2 Peter 1:10

The following will be just as real and definite as the coming, if there is any reality in you at all; and if you are not deluding yourself with a deceitful cloud-land of sentimental religion, without foundation and without substance, which is but a refuge of lies which the hail shall sweep away. Do not sit down in this most serious state of uncertainty, but "give diligence to make your calling and election sure."

Romans 6:2, 4, 13, 22; Matthew 4:18–20; 8:22; 9:9

But you say, "How am I to know whether I am following?" Well, following is not standing still. Clearly it is not staying just where you always were. You cannot follow one thing without coming away from something else. Apply this test. What have you *left* for Jesus? What have you left off doing for His sake? If you are moving onward, some

Philippians 3:13	things must be left behind. What are "the things which are behind" in *your* life? If the supposed coming has made no
Matthew 7:21	difference in your practical daily life, do not flatter yourself
2 Cor. 5:17	that you have ever yet really come at all. Jesus says, "If any
Matthew 16:24	man will come after Me, let him deny himself, and take up
Luke 14:27	his cross and follow Me." What light does that saying throw

Philippians 3:13

things must be left behind. What are "the things which are behind" in *your* life? If the supposed coming has made no difference in your practical daily life, do not flatter yourself that you have ever yet really come at all. Jesus says, "If any man will come after Me, let him deny himself, and take up his cross and follow Me." What light does that saying throw upon your case? Be honest about it; all true coming *to* Jesus must issue in thus coming *after* Him.

Then look at it from the positive side. He has left us "an example that ye should follow His steps." As the beautiful collect puts it, "Give us grace that we may daily endeavour ourselves to follow the blessed steps of His most holy life." Now, what are those steps? Perhaps you are not even looking to see what they are, let alone following them! Following the *steps* is quite a different thing from thinking to follow one's own idea of the general direction of a course. If you would only take one Gospel, and read it through with the earnest purpose of noting, by the Holy Spirit's guidance, what the steps of Jesus are, you would soon see clearly whether you are following or not, far more clearly than by reading any amount of books about it, or consulting any number of human counsellors. Take for to-day only one indication of what those steps were. "Who went about doing good." Do your steps correspond with that? It is not, "went about doing no harm," but actively and positively "doing good."

Oh, dear friends, they are "blessed" steps in all senses of the word! For His ways are ways of pleasantness, and all His paths are peace. Once fairly and fully entered, the paradox is always solved, the self-denial is lost in the greater joy of pleasing Him, the cross becomes a sceptre in the hand of His "kings and priests." Then you shall "continue following the Lord your God." And the end of the following is, "that where I am, there shall also My servant be."

Matthew 7:21
2 Cor. 5:17
Matthew 16:24
Luke 14:27

1 Peter 2:21

John 13:15

Psalm 63:8

Matthew 11:29

Acts 10:38
1 John 2:6

Proverbs 3:17

John 8:12
Philippians 3:7
Rev. 1:6; 1 Sam. 12:14; Jn. 12:26
Revelation 14:4

TWENTY-FIRST DAY.

"Coming with Jesus."

"Come with me"—Song of Solomon 4:8

Song. 2:10
Matthew 11:28
Matthew 16:24
2 Samuel 19:33
1 Cor. 1:26

Mark 3:14
Revelation 3:4, 21

John 6:68
Exodus 33:14

Proverbs 18:24

John 14:23

Hebrews 13:5

Numbers 23:19

Matthew 28:20
Psalm 91:15

" COME away" is not all that the Lord Jesus has to say to us. "Come unto Me" and "Come after Me" only lead up to the even more gracious invitation, "Come *with* Me."

"Ye see your calling"; it is nothing less than to come *with* Jesus. The enviable privilege of the twelve whom Jesus ordained "that they should be with Him," is freely offered to you. Will you avail yourself of it? Will you come with Jesus, walking with Him from this day every step of the way? Will you accept Him as the Guide with whom you will go, the Friend with whom you will commune by the way? It will be no dreamy or nominal coming with Him, if only you are willing to come. You will find it very real in all respects.

You can never be so *really always* with any earthly friend as you can be with Jesus, and as you *will* be, if you accept the invitation. For there are two sides to that "with." If you will but *come with* Him, He will come unto you and *abide with* you. Your natural fear lest, even when you consent to come to be with Him, you might not remain with Him, is met and completely settled by His promise, "I will never leave thee." And of course, if He *never* leaves you, you will always be with Him. And if He has *said* that, of course He will do it. So do not let *that* objection come up again!

It is a very common experience in great things and small, that the person or thing we most want is not there just when we most want him or it. Never shall we have to complain of this as to the promised perpetual presence of our Lord; for He says, "I will be with him in trouble." "When thou

Isaiah 43:2
Psalm 23:4

Luke 13:34
Song. 5:2

John 17:24

Isaiah 63:9

1 Kings 18:21

John 6:67
Genesis 24
Genesis 23:6

Genesis 24:57, 58

passest through the waters, I will be with thee." And in the deepest need of all, in the valley of the shadow of death, the soul that has yielded to the present call will be able to say, "Thou art with me!"

I do not think we consider enough how we disappoint the love of Jesus when we refuse to come with Him. For He does truly and literally desire us to be with Him. Would He have made it the very climax of His great Prayer, representing it as the very culmination of His own rest and glory, that His people should be *with Him,* if He did not so very much care about it, and was only seeking and saving us out of bare pity? No, it was in His *love* as well as in His pity that He redeemed us! And love craves nearness. This is the very thing that differences love from the lesser glow of mere pity, or kindness, whatever their degrees or combinations. The Lord Jesus would not say, "Come *with* Me," if He did not feel towards us something far beyond any degree of pity and kindness. It is the Royal Invitation of His kingly love.

But now, what are you going to do about it? Hearing it, and thinking it very gracious, and all that, is not enough. You must come to a point about it. You must give as definite an answer to this as mere common courtesy demands to any earthly invitation. Giving *no* answer is an acknowledged insult. Will you treat the King thus? And if not, what shall your answer be? You must give it yourself. Christ Himself is waiting for it.

There is a beautiful type which tells us how a maiden was chosen to be the bride of the son of "a mighty prince" in a far-off land. She was to answer for herself about it, and so "they said, We will call the damsel and enquire at her mouth. And they called Rebekah, and said, Wilt thou go with this man? And she said, *I will go.*"

Shall this be *your* answer to-day?

TWENTY-SECOND DAY.

―――――

The Living Water.

"If any man thirst, let him come unto Me, and drink,"—John 7:37.

THE Invitation could not have been given in any wider form. Neither could it have been given in any form which so certainly concentrates all its light and warmth on one point, that point yourself!

First, there is the grand sweep of the "*any*" man. Instead of amplifying this into a list of all possible varieties of "rich or poor, old or young," and so on, just never mind about these usual human paraphrases, which may or may not seem to include you, and come face to face with the magnificently simple word of our Lord, "Any!" and know that it means "*you!*" for you cannot possibly get outside of this great circle, described by the hand of Infinite Love. You cannot possibly say it does not include you. Words mean nothing, if this word does not mean that you, whose eyes now rest upon it, are included and intended. To you the Lord Jesus says, "Let him come unto Me."

But another word is appended which seems at first sight to be a limitation. "If any man *thirst,* let him come." *Is* it a limitation? Ask your own heart! Is there *any* one who does not thirst? In other words, is there any one who can say before God who searches the heart, "I am satisfied. I have no sense of thirst, no nameless craving"? Are *you* satisfied? I do not mean, are you tolerably contented and comfortable on the whole and in a general way when things are at their best? But, *satisfied!*—the deep under-the-surface rest and complete satisfaction of the very heart, the filling of its emptiness, the stilling of all its cravings; and this not during the false frothing of excitement or business, but when you are

Revelation 21:6
Psalm 107:5

Ezekiel 11:5

alone, when you lie awake in the night, when you are shut away from any fictitious filling of your cup, and when the

Jeremiah 2:13

John 2:25

broken cisterns have leaked out, as they will, and do, and must,—are you satisfied then? Verily, He who knew what was in man knew that He was not narrowing the invitation

Revelation 22:17

when He said, "Let him that is athirst, come!"

Did you ever think *why* it is so utterly hopeless and useless to try to quench that inner thirst with anything but the

Philippians 1:19

John 7:39

John 4:13

John 10:35

living water, "the supply of the Spirit of Jesus Christ"? He has said plainly and positively that you shall not succeed! He hath said, "Whosoever drinketh of this water *shall* thirst again." You see there is no chance for you, for His word cannot be broken, and He says you "*shall* thirst again." There are only two issues of that perpetual thirst. One is the unan-

Luke 16:24

swered entreaty for a drop of water, only so much as the tip of a finger may bear, not to quench the unquenchable thirst, but only to *cool* a flame-tormented tongue. The other, the

John 4:14

only other, is, "Whosoever drinketh of the water that I shall give him shall never thirst." And lest our slow perceptions should fail to grasp the fact in the figure, the Lord Jesus re-

John 6:35

Psalm 107:9

John 7:37

peats the promise, and says, "He that believeth on Me shall never thirst." Never! for "He satisfieth the longing soul."

"Let him come *unto Me,* and drink." You see there is only this one way of drinking of the living water: you must come to Jesus Himself, personally and really. Knowing all about it is not enough. Consulting Christian friends, and reading good books, and doing any amount of religious duties, and exercising any amount of self-denial, will not stay the more or less conscious heart-thirst. The Lord says not a word about any channels; He only says, "If any man thirst,

Revelation 22:17

let him come unto Me, and drink." And "Whosoever will, let him take of the water of life freely." Will not *you* come?

TWENTY-THIRD DAY.

The Bread and Wine.

"Come, eat of my bread, and drink of the wine which I have mingled."—Proverbs 9:5.

1 Cor. 1:24, 30

IN several chapters of Proverbs the Lord Jesus Christ is beautifully described under the figure of Wisdom. For He is "the Wisdom of God," and He is "made unto us Wisdom."

In this verse He gives a double Invitation,—to eat of His bread, and drink of His wine. These are the symbols of life and joy—His life and His joy.

"Come, eat of My bread." "Feed on Him in thy heart by faith, with thanksgiving." For Jesus Himself is the true Bread from heaven. And he that eateth of this Bread shall live for ever. For He is the Bread of Life, life-giving and life-sustaining.

John 6:32
John 6:48
Galatians 2:20

How shall we eat? It is the old story,—only coming, only believing! For "he that cometh to Me shall never hunger," and "we are made *partakers* of Christ, if we hold the beginning of our confidence stedfast unto the end."

John 6:35
Hebrews 3:14

It is not a mere tasting or a bare subsisting to which Christ invites us. He says, "Eat, O friends; drink, yea, drink abundantly, O beloved." For "I am come that they might have life, and that they might have it more abundantly"; fulness and vigour of life, abounding pulses of vitality, fresh and strong; life that shall not and cannot fail, for "He ever liveth," and "because I live, ye shall live also."

Song. 5:1
John 10:10

Hebrews 7:25
John 14:19
Luke 1:53
Luke 15:16
Isaiah 44:20
Jer. 31:14, 25
Psalm 107:9

How often we have sung, "He hath filled the hungry with good things!" Are you hungry? Come, eat of His bread, leaving the husks and ashes, and you shall know what it is to be filled with good things. For "He filleth the hungry soul with goodness."

It is not only the solid life-need of bread that is provided at the feast which the Lord has made for us, but Wine, the symbol of joy, "that maketh glad the heart of man." "Come, buy wine and milk without money and without price," because the price is already paid for it. His sorrow was the price of the joy offered to us. He poured out His soul unto death, that He might pour out His joy into our lives. He emptied the cup which His Father gave Him, that He might fill ours till it runs over. Without price to us,— but oh, the price to Him!

The Lord Jesus says it is wine which He has *mingled*. Not all one kind, but mingled by Divine care and skill into a perfect draught of manifold gladness. "If they obey and serve Him, they shall spend their days in prosperity, and their years in pleasures." *That* is the heritage of the servants of the Lord! Did you think it was so pleasant? Did you know that He meant you to spend your years in pleasures *here,* as well as to give you the pleasures for evermore hereafter? "Come, drink of the wine that He has mingled," and you will find out what these pleasures are, and how exceedingly real they are! No wonder you are a little sceptical about it! for "eye hath not seen, nor ear heard, neither have entered into the heart of man, the things which God hath prepared for them that love Him; but," notice now exactly what is said, "*God* HATH *revealed them unto us by His Spirit.*" So, unless or until God reveals them to you by His Spirit, you cannot see or conceive what these pleasures are which He has prepared for those who love Him,—what this wine is which He has mingled for those who come to Him. Oh taste and see! Come, and put your trust under the shadow of His wings; and *then* you shall be abundantly satisfied with the fatness of His house, and He shall make you drink of the *river* of His pleasures.

Psalm 104:15
Isaiah 55:1

Isaiah 53:12
John 15:11
John 18:11
Psalm 23:5

Job 36:11
Psalm 90:14
Isaiah 65:13, 14

Psalm 4:7
Proverbs 3:17
Psalm 16:11

1 Cor. 2:9, 10

Psalm 34:8
Psalm 36:7, 8
Psalm 63:5
Psalm 65:4

TWENTY-FOURTH DAY.

_____

Will You Not Come?

"Thou hast received gifts for men; yea, for the rebellious also."—Psalm 68:18.

John 5:40	WILL you not come to Him for life?
Ezekiel 33:11	Why will ye die, oh why?
John 10:11	He gave His life for you, for you!
Romans 6:23	The gift is free, the word is true!
2 Cor. 5:20	Will you not come? oh, why will you die?
Acts 10:36	Will you not come to Him for peace—
Colossians 1:20	Peace through His cross alone?
1 Peter 1:19	He shed His precious blood for you;
Romans 5:15, 18	The gift is free, the word is true!
Ephesians 2:14	He is our Peace! oh, is He your own?
Jeremiah 6:16	Will you not come to Him for rest?
Matthew 11:28	All that are weary, come!
Isaiah 11:10	The rest He gives is deep and true;
Isaiah 28:12	'Tis offered now, 'tis offered you!
Hebrews 4:3, 9	Rest in His love, and rest in His home.
Matthew 13:44	Will you not come to Him for joy,—
John 16:24	Will you not come for this?
Philippians 2:7, 8	He laid His joys aside for you,
John 15:11	To give you joy, so sweet, so true!
Romans 15:13	Sorrowing heart, oh, drink of the bliss!
Ephesians 3:19	Will you not come to Him for love—
Psalm 107:9	Love that can fill the heart,
Ephesians 2:4	Exceeding great, exceeding free?
Revelation 1:5	He loveth you, He loveth me!
Romans 5:8	Will you not come? Why stand you apart?

John 4:14	Will you not come to Him for *all?*
Psalm 34:8	Will you not "taste and see"?
Isaiah 30:18	He waits to give it all to you;
Matthew 7:7, 8	The gifts are free, the words are true!
John 7:37	Jesus is calling, "Come unto Me!"

TWENTY-FIFTH DAY.

Come Near.

"Come ye near unto Me."—Isaiah 48:16.

Zephaniah 3:2

" **S**HE obeyed not the voice; ... she trusted not in the Lord, she drew not near to her God." What was

Zephaniah 3:1
Hebrews 6:9
John 12:32

her portion? "Woe to her!"

"But, beloved, we are persuaded better things of you, though we thus speak." For Jesus says that if He is lifted up, He will draw all men unto Him. And it is the Lord Je-

Isaiah 48:16

sus Himself (see context) who says, "Come ye near unto Me, hear ye this!" No matter how far off you may be, this

Isaiah 57:19
Isaiah 48:18
2 Chron. 29:31

call of peace is to you who are far off. And if you hearken, then shall your peace be as a river. And if you have already come to Jesus, still He says to them that are nigh, "Now ye have consecrated yourselves to the Lord, come near,"—nearer still, closer and closer to the Lord who loves you.

Hebrews 10:19

There is only one way of coming near or being made near, but that way is open for you. Not into the outer court of religious professions, but "into the Holiest," into the reality of most sacred nearness to your Lord, you may enter "by the blood of Jesus." The moment you claim by faith

Hebrews 13:12
Leviticus 14:14
Hebrews 9:13, 14
Ephesians 2:13
Hebrews 4:14
Romans 5:9
Ephesians 3:12
Heb. 10:21, 22

the power of that precious blood,—the moment you let your Great High Priest put it upon you, that moment "ye who sometimes were far off are made nigh by the blood of Christ." Then, having this High Priest, and having this one blessed and unfailing means of access, "let us draw near with a true heart, in full assurance of faith."

Isaiah 33:13
Eph. 2:13, 17
1 Peter 1:19

Do not be discouraged from coming near because you feel far off. Take that rather as your very claim to be included in the call, for He says, "Hear, ye that are far off, what I have done!" and take it as your very reason for coming;

Luke 15:20
Zechariah 6:15

come just because you *are* "a great way off," for He says, "They that are far off shall come."

If you feel very powerless about it, plead and claim the promise of His enabling grace, "I will cause him to draw near." And then you will find that "blessed is the man whom Thou choosest, and causest to approach unto Thee"; and your experience will be, "It is good for me to draw near unto God."

Jeremiah 30:21
Psalm 65:4

Psalm 73:28

He who causes you to come near will keep you near. Joseph did not only say to his brethren, "Come near to me," in that moment of tenderest love when he made himself known to them, but his promise was, "And thou shalt be near unto me." This is your calling. Never to be far off any more! Never any more distance and separation! Never any more wandering in the far country without God, but henceforth to be "a people near unto Him!" "No more strangers and foreigners, but fellow-citizens with the saints, and of the household of God," having found the very home of the weary heart, from which you shall no more go out.

Genesis 45:4

Genesis 45:10

Romans 8:35–39
Luke 15:13; Eph.
2:12; Ps. 148:14
Ephesians 2:19

Revelation 3:12

TWENTY-SIXTH DAY.

To the Uttermost.

"But this man, because He continueth ever, hath an unchangeable priesthood. Wherefore He is able also to save them to the uttermost that come unto God by Him."— Hebrews 7:24, 25.

"**A**ND suppose I do come, what then? Suppose I do receive all this blessedness to-day, what about to-morrow?" Something like this thought is very often in the minds of those who see the lions not only outside but inside the doors of the House Beautiful. But it is all met by that wonderful word, "to the uttermost."

Psalm 130:1
Acts 1:8

This does not only mean that the Lord Jesus is able to save out of the uttermost depth of need and misery and sin, and that He is able to save from the uttermost regions of distance and despair. It means all that, but more besides. It is

Psalm 40:2

not only bringing you up out of the horrible pit and miry clay, but setting your feet upon a rock, and establishing your goings.

Eccles. 3:14
Isaiah 45:17
Jeremiah 17:14

The word is one of those remarkable compound ones for which we have no equivalent. It means that He is able to save unto all completeness, unto the total perfection of saving.

Suppose I were drowning, and you drew me out of the deepest water, just in time to save my life, but then left me wet and shivering and exhausted on the bank, to run the more than risk of wretched after-effects of cold and rheumatism, from which I might never entirely recover! That would not be saving "to the uttermost" in this sense of the word. But if you did the thing completely,—carrying me home, and doing everything necessary to restore me, and avert ill effects, and that effectually; never relaxing in care and effort, nor letting me go, till you had me safe and well, however long and difficult it might be, then you would have saved me "to the uttermost," in the true meaning of it.

This is what Jesus is able to do for you. Your first coming to Him is only like letting Him grasp you in your terrible danger, and draw you out of the fatal depths. But "because He continueth ever," always the same loving and faithful Saviour, He will complete what He begins. For we are "confident of this very thing, that He which hath begun a good work in you will perform it until the day of Jesus Christ." Having saved you from destruction, His very name is the guarantee that He will not leave you to struggle helplessly with your sins, much less to "continue" in them, but that He shall save you from them. You will find it a daily continual salvation, by which He will keep you by the power of God through faith, unto the consummated salvation of body and soul, "ready to be revealed in the last time."

Hebrews 7:24
1 Thess. 5:24
Philippians 1:6

Matthew 1:21

Romans 6:1
Psalm 103:3–5
2 Peter 1:4
1 Peter 1:5

TWENTY-SEVENTH DAY.

The Proof of Christ's Ability to Save.

"Wherefore He is able also to save them to the uttermost that come unto God by Him, seeing He ever liveth to make intercession for them."—Hebrews 7:25.

SEE what is the proof that the Lord Jesus Christ is able to save you thus, "to the uttermost." It is that He ever liveth to make intercession. For whom? For them "that come unto God by Him." Or, as He Himself said, in that wonderful prayer when He lifted the veil from His own Divine communing with the Father, and let us hear His mighty intercession: "Neither pray I for these alone, but for them also which shall believe on Me through their word,"— thus again identifying "coming" with believing. Then, if you come, the perpetual intercession of our ascended High Priest will be for you, always for you. Only think that this is what Jesus is now living for,—"liveth to make intercession" for you! Should we ever have dared to imagine such grace and love? Should we ever have conceived that such a privilege could be ours?

Only think what security there must be in it! If the Lord Jesus is praying for you, can you perish? If He is praying for you, will not the Father's answer of blessing be beyond anything you would ask for yourself? Is not this enough to answer all your misgivings as to what you will find and how you will get on when you have come?

There is a solemn side to it. He not only says nothing about making intercession for those who do *not* come, but He plainly and positively says, "I pray *not* for the world, but for them which Thou hast given Me"; the proof of having been *given* to Christ being the *coming* to Him, for "all that the Father giveth Me shall come to Me." Then face the terrible position which is yours if you will not come! Christ will

John 17:20

Hebrews 4:14
Romans 8:34
Hebrews 7:25

John 10:28

John 17:9

John 6:37

not pray for you! you shut yourself out from the prayer of Him whom the Father heareth *always*. He prays *not* for all alike, but only for those who receive His words. He says, "I pray for them; I pray *not* for the world." You dare not and cannot explain this away. It is no mere inference, no question of differing "views," but spoken by Him whose words can never pass away. Will you not "come," and share in this unspeakable privilege of Christ's intercession?

We must not overlook the fact that it is for those who "come unto God by Him." Your coming to Jesus is also coming to your Father. In our right earnestness to have clear views of the Trinity, we are liable to forget the *Unity* of the Godhead. "I and My Father are one," saith the Lord Jesus; and this blessed and glorious unity is our key to many an apparent difficulty. Yet there is a Divine order in the approach, which we invert at our eternal peril. It must be "by Him," or it is no coming at all. For He hath said, "No man cometh unto the Father but by Me." The redemption of Christ is for them "who *by Him* do believe in God." You *cannot* be made nigh to God except by the blood of Christ. You *cannot* reach the Father except through the Son, for it is through Him and in Him that we alone have access. You *cannot* offer thanks, any more than prayer, to God, except in the same way, for it is "by Him" that we are to offer it. In one word, you cannot be saved any other way at all, except by Jesus, and it is no use talking about being simply saved by God's mercy, for God's own Word says, "There is none other name under heaven given among men whereby we must be saved," so that fallacy is disposed of for ever. So "diminish not a word"; do not venture to leave out the words "by Him," but come in God's own appointed way, and you shall be saved in His own grand and perfect way, "to the uttermost!"

John 11:42

Luke 21:33

John 10:30

John 14:6

1 Peter 1:21
Ephesians 2:13

Ephesians 2:18

Hebrews 13:15
Romans 5:9, 10
Acts 13:39
Acts 4:12

Deut. 12:32
Jeremiah 26:2

TWENTY-EIGHTH DAY.

Continual Coming.

"To whom coming, as unto a living stone, disallowed indeed of men, but chosen of God, and precious, ye also, as lively stones, are built up a spiritual house, an holy priesthood, to offer up spiritual sacrifices, acceptable to God by Jesus Christ."—1 Peter 2:4.

Matthew 7:14

" To whom *coming.*" Here is the secret of advance in the narrow way, after we have entered by the Strait Gate. It is not the having come once and to begin with, but the coming continually to Jesus. When we have once really come to Him, it is not only our privilege, but our constant joy, to come to Him about everything—to go on drinking at the fountain. It is a beautiful paradox which is realized and reconciled in the experience of those who come, that we may be continually coming afresh without ever going away,—always *at* the fountain-head, and yet always *coming* to it.

1 Cor. 3:11

As the first coming to Jesus gives us the true and only foundation, so by the very same coming, continued with ever fresh peace and joy, we shall be built up in Him. It is

Colossians 2:6, 7
1 Peter 2:5

as we have received Christ Jesus the Lord that we are to walk in Him, and then we shall be rooted and built up in Him. Think what this building up implies! Coming to Him, you individually, as well as all who come collectively, shall be

Ephesians 2:22
Ephesians 3:17
1 Cor. 6:19

builded together for an habitation of God through the Spirit, that Christ may dwell in your hearts by faith, that your bodies may be the temple of the Holy Ghost. Coming to

Jeremiah 12:16

Him, you shall no longer be a loose stone, lying about and getting weatherworn, but you " shall be built in the midst of My people," saith the Lord.

1 Peter 2:5, 9
Revelation 1:5, 6
Revelation 5:10

Coming to Him, you shall also be built up as a holy and royal priesthood. For He that loved us and washed us from our sins in His own blood, hath made us kings and priests unto God. What does this priesthood involve, which the Lord has "given unto you as a service of gift"? Does it not involve the very point on which you had a misgiving, namely, "If I do come to-day, what about to-morrow?" for the priests had everything provided for them. When they were set apart to the priest's office, they did not need to have a thought or a care about their maintenance in it all the rest of their lives. When once this "service of gift" was theirs, they were joined unto the high priest himself, and shared his privileges and his provision; they were given to him, and he was given to them. This provision for them was "all the *best* of the oil, and all the *best* of the wine, and of the wheat, and the first-fruits," besides "all the *best* thereof" of other things; "for it is your reward for your service." And the Lord says, "I will satiate the soul of My priests with fatness." They shall be abundantly "satisfied with the plenteousness of Thy house." For "His divine power hath given unto us *all* things that pertain unto life and godliness."

Coming to Him, you shall "offer up spiritual sacrifices, acceptable to God by Jesus Christ." You will offer by Him the sacrifice of praise continually; and what can the angels do more? Continual praise *must* be continual gladness. And when you are able to say, "O Lord, I will praise Thee; though Thou wast angry with me, Thine anger is turned away, and Thou comfortedst me; behold, God is my salvation"; then, and "*therefore*, with joy shall ye draw water out of the wells of salvation."

This is what is before you, as soon as you come to Jesus. Thenceforth it shall be continual coming, and that will be continual rest, continual peace, continual joy.

Numbers 18:7

Numbers 18:9, 14

Ezekiel 44:28–30
2 Cor. 6:10
Numbers 18:2, 4

Numbers 18:12

Num. 18:29, 31

Jeremiah 31:14
Ps. 36:8, P.R.V.
2 Peter 1:3

1 Peter 2:5;
Romans 12:1
Hebrews 13:15
Ps. 71:6, 14; 34:1
Isaiah 12:1–3

Philippians 4:4, 6, 7

TWENTY-NINTH DAY.

Fellowship and Cleansing.

"Come ye, and let us walk in the light of the Lord."—Isaiah 2:5.

Revelation 22:17

Numbers 10:29
Jeremiah 50:5
Hosea 6:1; Heb.
4:16

2 Cor. 5:14

Isaiah 2:5

John 8:12

1 John 1:7

1 John 3:14

1 John 1:3

IT is not only the Spirit but the Bride who says, "Come." And it is remarkable that the Bride is never found saying "Come" without including herself. "Come with *us*"; "Come, and let *us* join ourselves unto the Lord"; "Come, and let *us* return unto the Lord"; "Let *us* come boldly." It is always "us," expressed or implied, though the speaker be patriarch, prophet, or apostle. And you may be very sure that those who venture to "say, Come" to you, are truly and deeply feeling the need of continual coming for themselves. If the Master's call were not sounding very fresh and sweet in their own hearts, they would not be constrained to sound it out to you.

"Come ye," then, "and let us walk in the light of the Lord." This is one of the blessed results and tests of true following, as following is of coming. For the Lord says, "He that followeth Me shall not walk in darkness, but shall have the light of life." And the results of this walking in the light are fellowship and cleansing; and these, when fully accepted, are all that we can need for the brightest, happiest pilgrim course. "If we walk in the light, as He is in the light, we have fellowship one with another; and the blood of Jesus Christ His Son cleanseth us from all sin." This is not merely fellowship with other Christians, though that, with all its warmth and pleasantness, is no doubt included. But scholars tell us that the true meaning is that we and the Lord have fellowship *with each other*—a marvellous mutual interchange of sympathy, interest, and love. "Truly our fellowship is with the Father, and with His Son Jesus Christ." Fellowship implies a good deal more than even friendship;

the word is really "communion," in its widest and yet closest sense. It is literally having all things in common. It is the Lord saying, "Thou art ever with Me, and all that I have is thine." It is our responding, "My Beloved is mine, and I am His." It is, "All are yours, and ye are Christ's, and Christ is God's." It is the present fact, which yet we cannot fully apprehend, till "at that day ye shall know that I am in My Father, and ye in Me, and I in you." "Come ye, and let us walk in the light of the Lord," that this glorious fellowship may be ours.

But there can be no fellowship without the cleansing. For how "can two walk together, except they be agreed?" And sin is the one great obstacle to this agreement. God never makes peace with sin. No armistice, no truce, no compromise is possible! If you would read through Jeremiah or Ezekiel with your eyes open to observe what God thinks of sin, you would be perfectly startled. It leaves the impression that no language can convey His indignant loathing of "this abominable thing which I hate." But this one precious promise shows it all in a moment. "The blood of Jesus Christ His Son cleanseth us from all sin!" If anything less than the blood of His own Son *could* have cleansed us, would He not have spared Him? Nothing shows us the exceeding sinfulness of sin like this one word.

But oh, thank God for the "all"! As nothing less than the blood of Christ is needed for one single sin, so nothing more is needed for *all* sin. Ask the Holy Spirit to open out this one word to you. "All" the sin cleansed by it,—"all" that separated between you and God put away by it,—you yourself made nigh by it, and sanctified by it,—the fellowship will be unbroken, the light will be unclouded, the following will be faithful, and the coming will be sealed.

Luke 15:31
Song. 2:16
1 Cor. 3:22, 23
Philippians 3:12
John 14:20
Isaiah 2:5
Genesis 5:22
Revelation 3:4

Amos 3:3
Psalm 66:18

Jeremiah 44:4
1 John 1:7

Romans 8:32

Hebrews 9:22

Psalm 119:19
Isaiah 59:2

Ephesians 2:13
Hebrews 13:12
Ephesians 5:8
Zechariah 10:12

THIRTIETH DAY.

The Perpetual Covenant.

"Come, and let us join ourselves to the Lord in a perpetual covenant that shall not be forgotten."—Jeremiah 50:5.

1 Cor. 6:17
Numbers 18:2
Romans 8:39
Ephesians 5:30
John 17:23
Jeremiah 50:5

Matthew 22:29

Hebrews 8:10

Jeremiah 31:32
Hebrews 8:9

Romans 3:19, 23

Isaiah 38:14

Jeremiah 31:33

2 Cor. 6:16
Revelation 21:3

Deut. 33:29

THIS is no external joining of church or congregation. "He that is joined unto the Lord is one spirit." To this we are invited,—to be so joined that nothing shall separate; to be made one with Christ in blessed and eternal union. The instrument, so to speak, of the joining, is our consent, in faith and obedience, to the perpetual covenant that shall not be forgotten.

Herein lies the answer to all the distressing doubts about persevering in which we "err, not knowing the scriptures, nor the power of God." For see what the terms of the new covenant are! "I will put My laws into their mind, and write them in their hearts: and I will be to them a God, and they shall be to Me a people." This seems all one-sided. It is all what God undertakes to do. Not a word about what we undertake to do. How different from any human covenant!

Ah, the Lord tried us with the other way, and we failed; and so the old covenant of works came to naught. It was not only the children of Israel who "continued not" in God's covenant; we have done just the same. We have proved in our own experience that we cannot keep any one condition of it, let alone the whole! And so the Lord makes a new covenant, in which the marvellous terms are that He undertakes our part as well as His own, by promising to put His laws into our minds and write them upon our hearts, so that we may keep them and really obey them.

And when He says He will be to us a God, He has promised in that one word more than mortal thought or mortal desire can reach. And when He says we *shall* be to Him a people, He guarantees us all the safety and happiness, and all the privileges and blessings, in all certainty and perpetuity, which He promises to His people. He knows our total weakness, and our utter inability to persevere, and so He stoops to undertake the whole thing for us, if we will only "come, and join ourselves to the Lord," consenting to His perpetual covenant, and accepting these wonderful provisions in simple faith.

But remember, there is no such thing as drifting into this covenant. We shall never "happen" to find ourselves included in it by waiting to see what turns up, or by dint of admiringly contemplating it. We must "*come*"; and we must join ourselves to the Lord in it by our own voluntary act and deed. Each must "subscribe with his hand unto the Lord." This covenant requires the free individual signature of each participator, so that each shall be able to say, "Yet hath He made with *me* an everlasting covenant, ordered in all things and sure." Do you ask for some proof that you *may* thus come and share its blessedness?—some distinct evidence that the covenant is meant for you? The Lord, who has given all the rest, has given this too. You know the freeness of the call, "Ho, *every one* that thirsteth, come ye to the waters." That is only the beginning of the Invitation. It goes on, without a break, still to *every* one,—"Incline your ear, and come unto Me; hear, and your soul shall live; and I will make an everlasting covenant with *you!*"

Oh, happy day that fixed my choice
  On Thee, my Saviour and my God!
Well may this glowing heart rejoice,
  And tell its raptures all abroad.

'Tis done! the great transaction's done:
  I am my Lord's, and He is mine;
He drew me, and I followed on,
  Charmed to obey the Voice Divine.

DODDRIDGE.

Margin references:
- 2 Cor. 1:20
- Psalm 103:14
- 119:117; Jude 24
- 2 Cor. 8:5
- Romans 7:4
- 2 Chron. 34:31
- Isaiah 44:5
- 2 Samuel 23:5
- Isaiah 55:1
- Isaiah 55:3

THIRTY-FIRST DAY.

The Consummation of the Invitation.

"Then shall the King say unto them on His right hand, Come, ye blessed of My Father, inherit the kingdom prepared for you from the foundation of the world."—Matthew 25:34.

Titus 2:13
Matthew 24:30, 31; 25:32, 34

" THEN!" when the sure but as yet unseen hope of the Church is fulfilled, and Jesus comes in His glory: "then!" when all are gathered before Him, and "He shall separate them one from another:" "*then* shall the King say unto them on His right hand, Come!"

Acts 1:11
Job 19:27

The King—"this same Jesus," who now says, "Come unto Me," "whom I shall see for myself, and mine eyes shall behold, and not another" (margin, *not a stranger*)—He shall

Luke 4:22
Isaiah 52:6
Matthew 11:28
Psalm 55:22
Psalm 38:4

utter with His own gracious lips the same sweet call; and we shall hear it, no longer by faith, but literally.

The call will be no longer, "Come unto Me, all ye that are weary and heavy laden"; for the weariness and the burdens that have been cast upon Jesus will be at an end for ever. It will be, "Come, ye blessed!" Not "blessed" then for the first time, but "ye" whose position already is that

Psalm 115:15
Ephesians 1:3

of "the blessed of the Lord." Every one who comes to Jesus takes that glorious position, and possesses all its manifold privileges. If you are only come today for the first time,

Genesis 26:29
Daniel 12:12, 13
Revelation 1:5, 6

"thou art *now* the blessed of the Lord," and you shall be among the blessed ones who stand in their lot at the end of the days. You are *now* made kings and priests unto God by Him who loved you and washed you from your sins in His own blood; and *then* the King will call you to "inherit the kingdom." For "by faith in Christ Jesus" (which is the

Galatians 3:26
Romans 8:17
1 Samuel 2:8
Revelation 3:21

same thing, in other words, as coming to Christ) , you are "the children of God." "And if children, then heirs; heirs of God, and joint-heirs with Christ." He will make you inherit the throne of His glory, and grant you to sit with Him

Luke 12:32
Ephesians 3:20

Matthew 25:46
Psalm 45:15

John 14:2
Hebrews 11:16
Matthew 25:34
Ephesians 1:4
1 Peter 1:4, Gr.
1 Peter 1:5

Revelation 5:10
John 6:37

in His throne, for it is your Father's good pleasure to give you the kingdom. Confess now, that this is doing for you exceeding abundantly above all you asked or thought! To be permitted just to escape the terrible doom of " everlasting punishment,"—just to get inside the door of the palace,—a sort of standing afar off, even in heaven—is about as much as you really thought of! But look at the grandeur of *His* thought, and the riches of His love for you! He has prepared not only "a place," and "a city," but a kingdom for you, and that not since you began to pray for salvation, but from the foundation of the world. And all this time this splendid and amaranthine inheritance has been reserved in heaven for you, and you are being kept by the power of God for it! Have you thanked Him for this? It is not too soon to do so.

This is indeed the consummation of the Royal Invitation,—the King on the throne of His glory inviting you to come and reign with Him!

And "this same Jesus" says to you to-day, "Him that cometh to Me, I will in no wise cast out."

Still shall the keyword ringing, echo the same sweet
    "Come!"
"Come" with the blessed myriads, safe in the
    Father's home;
"Come!" for the toil is over; "come!" for the feast
    is spread;
"Come!" for the crown of glory waits for the weary
    head.

Wayside Chimes. May.

Love for love.

"We have known & believed the love that God hath to us." I John 4. 16

Knowing that the God on high,
    With a tender Father's grace,
Waits to hear your faintest cry,
    Waits to show a Father's face,—
Stay & think! oh should not you
Love this gracious Father too?

Knowing Christ was crucified,—
    Knowing that He loves you now
Just as much as when He died
    With the thorns upon His brow,—
Stay & think! oh should not you
Love this blessed Saviour too?

Knowing that the Spirit strives
    With your weary, wandering heart,
Who would change the restless lives,
    Sure & perfect peace impart,—
Stay & think! oh should not you
Love this loving Spirit too?

Frances Ridley Havergal

A fair copy autograph of "Love for Love" by F.R.H., written February 12, 1879. See
page vi.

www.ingramcontent.com/pod-product-compliance
Lightning Source LLC
Chambersburg PA
CBHW060652030426
42337CB00017B/2585